WOLVES and their PREY

Who's Guarding Our Nation's Wealth

ROBERT GATES

We dedicate this book to the millions of Americans who are tired of being taken advantage of economically and labeled incompetent by politicians, who constantly refuse to promote the will of the people.

The theory of True Conservatism is not based on one man's moral judgment. This theory is the collective thought of men and women who are willing to abide by our constitutional rule of law. The theory of True Conservatism is a multilateral idea; fashioned in a way to protect all Americans.

President Abraham Lincoln understood this line of reasoning. The secret to his success, as president, was he purposely surrendered his intelligence to the Constitution. The Constitution was his legal guide. He understood that the nature of our nation's economic existence depended on its evolving and governing powers.

BY ROBERT DANIEL GATES

TABLE OF CONTENTS

THE EVOLVING DOCUMENT

A FOREWORD BY BILL GATES

As a businessman I am aware of what happens when you sit on the sidelines of life. You cannot move forward or achieve your goals.

It's no different when it comes to winning a better future for yourself and your family. Originally, like most Americans, I did not appreciate the Constitution's rule of law, nor did I know how to apply it in a business like fashion.

Allow me to introduce myself, my name is Bill Gates. I am the C.E.O. of Microstar Revolution. I am not the great Bill Gates of Microsoft. Though, there are times when people ask me if we are kin. I jokingly answer, "Yes, we are." We both have similar technological backgrounds and interests. One of our main interests is how to make vital business information available to the public, through the use of modern technology.

This book was written to demonstrate to the American people that our Republican Democracy is not a 'spectator's sport'. Perhaps you are convinced that those in Washington are more interested in their re-election then in your future. This is why those who take the time to learn and apply the necessary vital business information have the power to take control of their economic destiny.

This book is based on the life experiences of Americans and the things done to them and their ancestors in the name of justice. It is also about the United States Constitution and how it has given my family and I the desire to move forward in our business ventures. Our hopes and economic dreams came to life once we understood our role as citizens as well as our financial responsibility to the Union.

INTRODUCTION: WOLVES
AND THEIR PREY

WHO'S GUARDING OUR NATION'S WEALTH?

Imagine you are fleeing from a vicious enemy that is much stronger than you. You know that this enemy is merciless, since it has slaughtered many of your friends and family, both economically and emotionally.

You have made many attempts to defeat this enemy, but it continues to consume your income. This enemy has been in existence for more than two hundred years and is affecting every area of your life. In this sense, Americans are being pursued by just such an enemy.

Suddenly, a rescuer appears and pledges to protect you and your family from this powerful and destructive force. Who is this devoted rescuer? It is the noble and evolving language within our Constitution.

Knowing that the noble language within the Constitution is our only realistic rescuer, we began our exhaustive research of more than ten years in the preparation of this text. We wanted to uncover the many economic and legal tools embedded within the Constitution to begin the task of restoring our nation's wealth.

As you read this book from cover to cover, you will be exposed to the devastating economic effects of this hidden enemy. This enemy is one of our nation's dirtiest kept secrets. This secret is being concealed by our lawmakers and is the chief cause of the economic disparity in this country. It is a hidden agenda that is responsible for the devastation within our social and economic infrastructure.

You will learn throughout this book that the enemy in question is the flawed Three-Fifths Compromise agreement. This enemy is not a physical entity, but a delusional passage written within our Constitution. It is the foundational language that assisted in the creation of this nation. Americans must become aware of the economic and emotional damage the Three-Fifths Compromise has on them and their descendents.

The Three-Fifths Compromise agreement is a concealed and fraudulent provision, which separates its citizens from their wealth and their honor. This enemy does not care about your skin color, nor does it care about your status in life. It was designed, and exists, for one purpose only, and that is to constitutionally consume your wealth.

On paper, the Three-Fifths Compromise appears to be a harmless addition to Article One of the Constitution. Whereas in actuality, this compromise provision is a wolf in sheep's clothing, devouring ones civil liberties and income at will. It wreaks havoc on our economy and destroys our nation's labor force. The Three-Fifths Compromise agreement has economically and psychologically linked all Americans to the aftermath of Slavery's past, and the divisive era of the Civil War.

Throughout this book, we will focus on three major challenges. The first will be to present to the people the constitutional tools necessary for their economic success. Secondly, we will demonstrate that there are constitutional laws purposely designed to hinder the economic process of the majority of American people. Third, we focus on teaching and promoting the fundamental theories of True Conservatism, upon which our Republican/ Democracy was assembled

The *Wolves* mentioned in the title of this book are those policymakers, who purposely misappropriate our nation's economic resources for their own personal gain. While the *Prey* is the unsuspecting, ill-informed citizen, who like sheep follow their captors down the road to economic uncertainty.

We will explain how Congress has allowed the citizens to become prey to the economic flaws that are deeply-rooted within the language of this compromise provision. The majority of our lawmakers are very much aware of the source that is causing the economic disparity among Americans. However, they will not lift a finger to resolve it.

For the first time in our nation's history, the negative economic effect of this compromise provision is being felt by all Americans, regardless of their ethnicity. The devastating economic effect of this compromise provision is being debunked and discredited by politicians. These politicians have a financial interest in keeping Americans in the dark over the methods being used to highjack our nation's resources.

This consumer's advocate handbook opens the Pandora's Box regarding our enemy the Three-Fifths Compromise agreement. It reveals how lawmakers use this provision to keep the majority of Americans from becoming educated and economically sound. "Wolves and Their Prey", is not like other book, which only complain about our nation's problems and never give realistic solutions.

We have made it our mission to make available constitutional fixes for each and every problem that we will present. More importantly, this text not only outlines the economic dilemma we face, but will show you how to meet your financial responsibilities to your family and to this nation.

GUARDING OUR NATION'S WEALTH?

"Wolves and Their Prey: Who's Guarding Our Nation's Wealth," is a consumer's advocate handbook, that is purposely designed to show Americans a new economic pathway to their prosperity.

This handbook will demonstrate to all Americans that the Federal Government, Wall Street and the private sector are not constitutionally responsible for your family's income, you are! By reading this book you will discover a revolutionary way to create wealth, regardless of your ethnicity or your station in life.

This chapter is based on our American way of life and how we, as a nation, can experience a new economic expansion. Therefore, for this economic growth to take place, Americans need to recognize the value of true wealth, which comes in many forms other than money.

Tired of Feeling Powerless?

The mission of this book is to show Americans that to become economically sound, one must be prepared to share power, economic resources and the responsibility of governing this nation. Our objective is to demonstrate that both our lives and our economic wellness are ingrained within the provisions of our Constitution.

This book was also written for those who are tired of feeling powerless, and who want to get involved in reshaping our nation's economic future. Within this book are proactive methods that will allow us to debate and, at the same time, resolve our economic problems.

> "The problem of social organization is how to set up an arrangement under which greed will do the least harm, capitalism is that kind of a system."
>
> **Milton Friedman**

Most importantly, this book is about our rescuer, the Constitution. This Constitution is a trinity of theories. It was intentionally designed to be a timeless, living, and compassionate document. It was intended to focus on the fundamental theory of True Conservatism, while at the same time promoting the will of the people.

The theory of True Conservatism is both pro-State and in favor of a smaller, but effective Federal Government. The original goal of the theory of True Conservatism was to establish a form of liberty that would endure any issue of dissent. True Conservatism is a celebration of our country's governing charter and the foundation upon which all generations of Americans can place their trust.

Is This Book Fair and Balanced?

To make this book credible and insightful, as well as fair and balanced, it is written in part by four proud Americans. Debi Veaudry, a Caucasian American in her fifties, was born and raised in Southern California. Debi is a High School Instructional Assistant for Special Education. She is a proud Democrat and is a firm believer in a united front.

Armando Garcia, age 66 an American of Mexican descent, was born and raised in Southern California. Armando served 20 years in the military with two tours in Vietnam. He is retired and enjoys educating those who are less fortunate. At the age of 50 he decided to register as a non partisan, because of his philosophy of shared sacrifice.

> *"For time and the world do not stand still. Change is the law of life. And those who look only to the past or the present are certain to miss the future."*
>
> **John F. Kennedy**

Bill Gates, a 53 year old American of African descent, was born and raised in Gary Indiana. He now lives in Hawaii since having separated from the military. He is an entrepreneur, always seeking ways to earn revenues for his family and his friends. He is a libertarian with the philosophy that the Federal Government's role is to serve both the state and its citizens.

Last we have Robert Gates, a 55 year old American of African descent, who was born and raised in Gary, Indiana. He moved to Southern California at the age of 26. He is a single parent whose occupation is a Technical Consultant. At age 50 he became a Republican who believes in effective government.

These Americans come from different backgrounds, are of different ages, are of different ethnic groups, and have different cultural values. They came together to write this manuscript with the hope of uniting a nation. These Americans also found that they had one thing in common, and that is, their belief in the fundamental theory of True Conservatism.

This theory entitles every citizen the privilege of dissent and also entitles each individual the right to earn their prosperity. As guardians of the Constitution, these authors are exercising their constitutional privilege of opposition to the dreadful economic and psychological effects of the Three-Fifths Compromise agreement. This book is an inspirational tale of how these four Americans view the true image of America and her greatness.

Our Constitution's true purpose is to enable us to create economic wellness and success for ourselves, as well as for others. As authors, we believe in the noble language of the Constitution. As citizens, we place our trust in its true intent.

This text will be the nation's first constitutional consumer's advocate handbook.

> "Well first of all, tell me, is there some society you know of that doesn't run on greed? You think Russia doesn't run on greed? You think China doesn't run on greed? What is greed?
>
> **Milton Friedman**

It is designed to bring the language and the nature of our Constitution to a level where Americans can easily grasp its fundamental economic impact on their lives.

Illusionary Debates

The task of this book is to show Americans that to gain economic wealth; one must be willing to learn the laws that govern their economic existence. In addition, it will be shown throughout this book why both political parties persist on using the illusion of race in their debates over our national debt, slavery's past, and the anguish of the Civil War. Our analysis shows that both parties have failed to comprehend the complete economic and psychological harm being done by these illusionary debates.

Due to unproductive and misleading debates on race, lawmakers are incapable of developing new non-discriminatory laws. We have studied these cultural debates and found them to be biased, excluding various segments of the population from their conversations.

In our examinations of past injustices, it became increasingly clear that our political leaders are dismissing the economic and psychological impact that the Civil War and the aftermath of Slavery is having on our Confederate brothers and sisters. It was the ancestors of these men and women who also bled and died in establishing this nation.

Our research shows that we cannot continue to make these same constitutional mistakes in our efforts to make the descendants of slavery's past economically whole, without doing the same for those impoverished Caucasian descendants of the Civil War as well.

This text will validate the fact that the victims of Slavery's past and the victims of the Civil War are constitutionally, economically and culturally interrelated. Because of this research, it became obvious to us that, as a multi-ethnic nation, the only proactive way to bring about realistic economic fairness is to introduce bold new economic plans. These plans will reshape how commerce and wealth should function in this nation. You may be asking, how is this possible? How can the Constitution bring about economic wellness for all Americans?

The Graceful Effects of Our Constitution

....Our Constitution was designed to create a more ideal environment in which all ethnic groups could live in harmony and prosper. It sought to establish justice and insure domestic tranquility. It was also written to provide for the common defense, including promoting the general welfare of its citizens. Plus, it was designed to secure the blessings of liberty for us and that of our descendants.

The benefits and the graceful effects of our Constitution are not only designed for America, it was also intended to aid mankind as well. As you proceed with your examination of this book, you will discover that the tools for your economic success' are well within the Constitution's intent. You will also discover there are some articles within this document that were designed to deny wealth to some Americans. It is these inexcusable articles that we are addressing.

It is up to each American to redefine, examine and reshape how they will use these constitutional rules that govern them. More importantly, we as citizens are called upon by the Constitution, to not only be right in our hearts and fair-minded in our thinking, but to also be the guardians of our nation's wealth. These responsibilities are constitutional gifts granted to us at birth.

> "Let's talk sense to the American people. Let's tell them the truth, that there are no gains without pains, that we are now on the eve of great decisions, not easy decisions".
>
> **Adlai Stevenson**

Sharing of this Nation's Resources

Originally, we planned to write this book for our family members and friends. Our goal was to make a self-help book giving our families and friends a new economic perspective on life. After ten years of exhaustive research on the economic benefits of the Constitution, we recognized that it is the citizens who are ethically accountable for our nation's economy, not Congress.

With this significant information in hand, we knew that this wealth of information was too vital not to share with others. We also recognized that what we had uncovered would economically benefit all Americans, regardless of their ethnicity or their position in life.

The bottom line is; many of our politicians refuse to accept the fact that we are a multi-ethnic society. In addition, the sharing of this nation's resources and its responsibilities is the lawmaker's constitutional duty. Unfortunately, our legislators have failed and refused to reflect or to promote the multi-ethnicity of America. Collectively, we are all members of this nation and whatever negatively distresses one ethnic group will ultimately, in time, affect all of us.

Each one of us is responsible for comprehending and appreciating the rules and the laws that govern our economic outcome. The reader must not rely solely on politicians, or their government, to always solve their personal economic problems.

However, to continue to be a prosperous nation, additional financial and educational programs should be designed and implemented by Federal and State Governments. This, in turn, would allow the disadvantaged to easily participate within our nation's economic and political systems.

We must also understand that the price of freedom is maintained by our vigilance. As citizens, we are legally and morally obligated to assist our lawmakers in the corrections of past wrongs that have been committed in the name of justice.

Constitutional Language

The most difficult task in the writing of this book was in the personalization of the language within the Constitution. It became imperative for us to make these constitutional words come alive within the hearts and souls of all Americans. We want citizens to become aware that it is their responsibility to participate in the restoration of this country's economy. There-

> "No one's hiring. The job market sucks. I'm paying my rent with credit cards"
>
> **Lucy, 29 year old law school graduate**

fore, each chapter has been written in a user friendly format with the hope that self awareness will emerge among Americans. Included within this book are realistic answers to our everyday problems.

This chapter, "Who's Guarding our Nation's Wealth", allows Americans of all ages and ethnic groups to reflect upon the original purposes and perspectives on the systems of laws that govern our lives. These reflections are crucial to the economic survival of our families and our nation. Any time the collective minds of the citizen's change for the better, it will cultivate the good we have in our country.

There are several documents written by man in which our lives are centered. The first was the Bible, inspired by deity. The second is the Constitution of the United States, inspired by man. The Framers were very much aware of their humanity, and that any document written by them would not be free of imperfections.

They were also aware that governing man's morality was both unconstitutional and impossible. For God did not give man the authority to govern another man's morality. For man is himself born corrupt. This is why the Founding Fathers included methods for amending the Constitution when these imperfections or defects were discovered.

It is fundamentally crucial for every American to become aware that failure to correct constitutional errors will put the freedom of all Americans at stake. We must understand that our lives and our economic wellness are ingrained within these constitutional provisions.

The greatest difficulty in being a citizen within a republican /democracy is in the willingness to share power, wealth and responsibility. This is the corner-stone of our nation's achievements. Our economic way of life will become less difficult as more Americans

> "The Great Depression, like most other periods of severe unemployment, was produced by government mismanagement rather than by any inherent instability of the private economy."
>
> **Milton Friedman**

begin to proactively learn to use the economic tools contained within the Constitution.

Within the heart of our economy, resides a menacing foe, a constitutional defect. This defect threatens both our economic stability and our social infrastructure. This defect is the Three-Fifths Compromise agreement. It is the enemy to our republic. It is a concealed agreement established within Article One of the Constitution.

The fraudulent language of this agreement invalidates part of Article One. The purpose of this compromise provision, within Article One, was to hide the connection between the Three-Fifths Compromise agreement and the continuing hi-jacking of Americans wealth.

This compromise passage allowed for the materialization of favoritism within the rule of law as well as within our society. Because of this compromise agreement, men and women are being governed by the supremacy of cultural common knowl-edge belief. This cultural approach to governing is an insult to our republican/ democracy. We are a multi-ethnic republic, and not a cultural state.

We, as authors, are firmly convinced that this compromise provision is an enemy to the American constitutional way of life. For over 200 years, Americans as a whole have been blind-sided by the hidden economic intent of the Three-Fifths Com-promise agreement. The objective of this compromise was to allow the status quo constitutional and cultural control over commerce, naturalization and taxation policies, well into the future.

Regardless of one's ethnicity, the majority of citizens are un-able to envision how this compromise provision is negativity af-fecting them. Throughout this book it will be revealed to you how this compromise provision is affecting every area of our society. Americans must open their eyes to see the true source of this nation's economic disorder. In order for that to happen, citizens must be willing to receive and to hear the truth so as to comprehend this constitutional defect.

There is an old saying that asks, "If a tree falls in the forest and no one hears it, does it make any noise?" The obvious answer to the question is, "yes", there were sound waves. Yet, if there is no ear to pick up on the sound and interpret it, no one hears it as a noise.

Citizens must interpret what they hear in today's politics and become receivers of what is known to be the truth. The fact of the matter is this compromise provision is an appalling constitutional act. The fact that some Americans do not want to hear the truth about this malicious compromise, does not mean that this corrupt act does not exist.

The reason most Americans do not see the dreadful effects of this compromise is because the language that conceals the dreadful effects within the Constitution was deceptive. This enemy, the compromise provision, is hidden in plain view, as though it was written with a pen of honor.

Our rescuer, the noble language of the Constitution, is the only clear pathway to our individual freedoms. It is the essence of our nation's well being. However, the language within The Three-Fifths Compromise agreement is the total opposite. It has blinded Americans of their economic responsibilities to the Union.

There is a story about a mining explosion in West Virginia. This explosion plunged the trapped men into total darkness. When the rescue team managed to get a light through to them, one of the young men finally said, "Well, why don't they turn on the light?" The others looked at him in amazement. It was then they realized that the explosion had blinded him. In the darkness, the young man did not know that he was blind. The light revealed to him, and to the others, that he was blind.

This book will reveal to the American people that they too have been plunged into total economic darkness by the Three-

Fifths Compromise provision. This unconstitutional passage leaves countless Americans both economically and psychologically existing in the dark.

We must not only be honest with ourselves, but we must also understand that many Americans refuse, or are unable, to let go of the dark side of this nation's past. Every citizen needs to open their eyes to the true facts about this compromise provision.

Our social and economic problems, which we refuse to face, have originated from within the Three-Fifths Compromise agreement. It is imperative that we find genuine solutions to the predicaments in which we continue to find ourselves. There is also an enormous need for serious dialogue on how to resolve these constitutional errors

We wake up every morning facing the same problems, and yet we seem to bury our heads in the sand hoping that our problems will miraculously go away. There is nothing more powerful than millions of Americans raising their voices, casting their votes and petitioning their state and Federal Government for economic change. This is how we will restore our nation's economy, one community at a time, one state at a time, one petition at a time.

We are absolutely confident that the tools and methods for recovering our nation's wealth reside within the pages of our rescuer, the noble parts of our Constitution. To benefit economically from this book, you must understand the role that you must play as an American citizen.

Constitutional Guardians

As citizens we are legally bound to be participants in the fine tuning of our Constitution. Our Civil Liberties and Due Process depend on us doing our job. However, both political parties have taken our right of guardianship and have made choices that only benefit the elite. It is the negative economic effects of this compromise provision that keeps Americans from reaching their full potential.

We will illustrate how this compromise provision came about and how we, as the guardians of the Constitution, can resolve its negative impact in a proactive and realistic manner. What good does it do for us, as individuals and as a nation, to publically state our opposition to these constitutional injustices, when we fail to make any attempts at correcting them?

> "A lot of people perceive the young generation to be unconcerned. But I think a lot of them do care about what's going on."
>
> **Barry Haul, 26 year old Free Lancer.**

Americans will face an economic future that will be unacceptable if we fail to stand together and do what is constitutionally right. We must debate and correct these past wrongs or we will allow the victims of these wrongs to be victimized once again. Except this time, the victimization will be because of our own inaction.

We can no longer continue to be anti-government or blame others for these past wrongs, since we have the constitutional tools to resolve them. The economic future of our country will depend largely on each and every ethnic group that desires to become a constitutional guardian. The initiatives we take upon ourselves to understand this dreadful and corrupt compromise provision will be determined by our vigilance.

This consumer's advocate handbook will concentrate on six of the most prominent and pressing issues of the day. Our analysis begins with: **Chapter Two, "The Crisis of True Conservatism"**, which is primarily intended to bring to light the lack of leadership within our political system. It will also expose how both political parties have rejected the theories of True Conservatism.

We will illustrate how the Republicans and Conservatives, along with the Democrats, Modern-Liberals, are playing the race card for political gains. They are using the illusion of race to create cultural problems as a way to acquire votes. Those who identify with these political parties are being deceived by the greatest public relations campaign in American history.

Chapter Three, "Is a Constitutional Apology for the Three-Fifths Compromise a Necessity?" This chapter begins with a series of proposals that clarify why a constitutional apology for the Three-Fifths Compromise is necessary. This compromise provision has psychologically and economically linked all Americans to Slavery's past and the Civil War era. The immoral effects of these defects are being felt throughout this nation.

It has become increasingly clear that when the founders inserted this compromise provision into Article One, parts of that Article became unconstitutional. This compromise is an Apartheid passage and thereby makes our Constitution partially dysfunctional.

The language of this compromise provision constitutionally excluded the Native Americans and three-fifths of all other persons from their civil liberties. The three-fifths of all other persons included in Article One, Section Two, Paragraph Three of the Constitution were the African slaves and their descendents. This compromise provision has also indirectly and economically affected impoverished European Americans and their descendants as well.

The status quo has never completely understood the economic and psychological impact that the Three-Fifths Compromise is having on their descendents. This compromise, as intended, has not failed in its design. But it has over reached its aim and is now affecting all Americans who freely come to these shores.

Chapter Four," Reverse Discrimination: The Boomerang Effect", reveals the source of reverse discrimination. Historically, reverse discrimination was primarily directed toward persons based on the color of their skin. Reverse discrimination is another painful element of the Three-Fifths Compromise agreement. What some Caucasian men are feeling today in the workplace with regard to discrimination is legitimate. However, the correct legal phrase for what they are presently experiencing is not reverse discrimination but cultural discrimination, functioning in reverse.

Chapter Five, "The Deception of Entitlement", will examine the incoherent and fraudulent nature of our country's policies on immigration, naturalization and taxation. This chapter will also focus on the unfairness and lack of equality within these taxation and representation practices. We will also show that in the summer of 1875, the United States Court's commissioned scientists to gather scientific evidence proving to the world that the white skinned, European in America was legally a separate race.

However, what was discovered by the scientific commission was that the courts were incorrect in their racial assignments. The European population of America is part of a sub-group of Caucasians that exists around the world. It was scientifically proven that the Caucasian population in America was part of a larger ethnic group of peoples with different skin colors. There are Caucasians born with dark brown skin with blue eyes to pale or white skin with brown eyes. The term *White* people should not be legally deemed a race unto itself, as it exists presently on today's national census.

Chapter Six, "The Cancer from Within", will expose three types of white collar crimes. The first of these crimes is the Three-Fifths compromise agreement, which is a Constitutional White Collar Crime. This fraudulent agreement is what prevented the descendants of American slaves, and impoverished American Caucasians, from initializing the process of assimilating into main stream society. It also barred these segments of the population from ever initiating intergenerational transfer of wealth for their descendants. The second of these white collar crimes are Governmental White Collar Crimes, which were perpetrated by both Presidents Abraham Lincoln and Andrew Johnson. The third type of White Collar Crimes are committed within the private sector.

Chapter Seven, "Irreversible Damage, What is Your Name?", will illustrate a form of constitutional abduction that has been buried deep within the language of the Constitution. This is the abduction of one's name or birthright. This governmental crime is not only constitutionally hidden, but it strips away a person's humanity. This abduction not only affects the victims, it is also affecting our nation's economic resources.

This chapter provides an overview of the key differences between one's slave name and one's true birthright. The victims of this abduction are forced to identify with characteristics that are European. This abduction is both a spiritual and a legal raping of a person's family name and their cultural traditions.

> *"The ignorance of one voter in a democracy impairs the security of all."*
>
> **John F. Kennedy**

Chapter Eight, "The Source of Hope and Honor", was written to convey to readers how each of us can obtain our vision of becoming economically and psychologically sound. We will illustrate how we must deal with the economic and psychological imperfections within ourselves and within our Constitution. Every person in this country is born into a legacy which they did not choose for themselves. Some legacies have brought forth economic hardships, while other legacies have allowed for the intergenerational transfer of wealth.

Finally, Chapter Nine: "Challenges for a Nation", will present our most pressing challenges for today and what solutions may be available for tomorrow. It will also demonstrate how to seize upon these constitutional imperfections, and change them into productive economic values. This can be accomplished through the use of the innovative legal and economic tools within the Constitution.

These brief descriptions of each chapter demonstrate that the Three-Fifths Compromise agreement is a major blunder within the writings of the Constitution. The negative effects of this compromise provision must be resolved before we are able to restore our nation's wealth and honor.

> "Scientific evidence has shown that a person's name does have an effect on one's attitude, which also influences one's health."

This compromise provision brings out the very essence of prejudice in all of us. We can only see along the prejudicial lines of our own cultural common knowledge. Let us be clear, that prejudices are an indication that we are either misinformed, or ignorant of the facts.

Every point of view that we hold strongly may be based on falsehoods that we experience. It is these falsehoods that make us intolerant to another's point of view. To be fair; it is human nature to be narrow-minded about that which we know the least. That is why, as guardians of our nation's wealth, we must take pride in our responsibilities. If we do not participate in our country's political system, we will forfeit to Congress our economic and legal rights.

We challenge you, the reader, with a call to action, to learn the truth about your rights and to demand economic changes. We must focus on understanding our rights as guaranteed by the Constitution. Americans must recognize that our political leaders continue to resolve our nation's problems with solutions created by the status quo.

While there are numerous constitutional errors that we have not mentioned, this is a good starting point. These constitutional flaws will not be resolved by one session of Congress, or by one Presidential term.

Our solutions to some of the most pressing challenges confronting our country presently are reasonable. We also understand that to have a productive debate dealing with cultural and economic challenges, it should not be about who is morally right or wrong. It should be based on what side is legally justified in asking for relief. These discussions must be based on legal issues alone. Americans should be angry with their lawmakers, who purposely make flawed decisions that affect the lives of millions of their constituents.

This manuscript is more than just a self-help book on the Constitution's rule of law. It is a guide to our economic wellness. It confirms to every individual residing on American soil of their constitutional responsibility to the Union.

Our Constitution is a living, timeless and compassionate document and not just words on a piece of parchment. It is not just the soul of America, but the best of America. It is the language of the Constitution that brings optimism to all who believe in its vision of becoming a more perfect Union. Our blessings of liberty were established by this life transforming document.

This consumer's advocate handbook will enable you to see the big picture and how the pieces of our lives fit within the framing of the Constitution. This new understanding will decrease the cultural strains among ethnic groups, which will assist us in bridging economic and educational gaps.

As citizens, we are the guardians of this Constitution and from its noble words stem the sources for hope and wealth. As authors, we will fail our most important duty to our country if we do not say that; no amount of wisdom in a Constitution can produce wise government. Some citizens view our Constitution with sanctimonious reverence. They consider it to be equal to the Ark of the Covenant, too Holy to be touched. They credited our fore-fathers wisdom to be more than human, and believe what was written to be beyond amending.

When amendments are made, they should be in-line with the essence of the conservatism theories in which the Constitution was conceived. Otherwise, the character and fashion of our republican/democratic form of government will be altered. We do not advocate frequent or untried changes to the Constitution, though this nation must investigate the harm being done by this poorly written compromise agreement.

The survival of any nation depends on the integrity of its laws. Our Constitution, even with its errors, has been able to maintain its integrity. It has passed the test of time and is now evolving with the people. And how does a nation show that it is attempting to uphold its integrity? By acknowledging its errors and doing all it can to make amends.

It is with the noble articles of the Constitution by which we will make our stand and defeat this enemy. The Three-Fifths Compromise agreement is this nation's adversary, placing most Americans in debtor's prison. We have the tools and weapons to defend ourselves from this adversary. Although we must take the time to learn how to use these constitutional tools in a businesslike manner.

THE CRISIS OF
TRUE CONSERVATISM

This chapter is an introduction to some of the basic facts and concepts regarding the crisis of our nation's economy and our cultural struggles. It will expose how both political parties are engaged in rejecting the fundamental theories of True Conservatism.

These theories are the foundation upon which our nation was founded, they are the cornerstone to Americans way of life. The purpose of this chapter is to define what the theory of True Conservatism should mean to the American people. It may be useful at this point to say; "The Crisis of True Conservatism" is not about which political party is morally right or wrong, it is about those who live their lives protecting our Constitutional rule of law.

We therefore urge you not to reach any conclusions regarding any particular issues without reading two or more chapters from this book. You will then be in a better position to evaluate

> *"If you put the federal government in charge of the Sahara Desert, in 5 years there'd be a shortage of sand."*
>
> **Milton Friedman**

the facts for yourself. You will also be able to see this nation's economic and social problems from a business-like perspective. Only then can you make a clear judgment about what courses of action are necessary to move this nation forward, both collectively and economically.

This chapter will expose why there is a lack of leadership within our government. It will also reveal the methods being used by both political parties in the hijacking of our nation's wealth. Citizens who identify themselves as Republican, Conservatives, Democrats, Modern-Liberals, or members of the Tea Party, have little or no concept of the significance of the theory of True Conservatism. They are being deceived and blinded by the greatest public relations campaign in American history.

Both parties, with the assistance of their pundits and strategists, are suppressing the will of the people through the use of the concealed language within the Three-Fifths Compromise agreement. It is this language that constitutionally excluded Native Americans, women and three-fifths of all other persons of their civil liberties and their wealth. The three-fifths of all other persons confirmed in Article One, Section Two, Paragraph Three of the Constitution were the African slaves and their descendents.

This compromise provision continues to impair millions of Americans economically. The language within this compromise provision is in total opposition to what the theory of True Conservatism stands for. To this degree, the language within the compromise provision utilizes the illusion of race and cultural profiling as its foundation. Americans cannot have any productive debates on the restoration of our nation's wealth, without attending to the destructive patterns of this flawed Three-Fifths Compromise agreement.

Re establishing True Conservatism

The status quo must understand that their descendents are also being economically and emotionally impaired by the Three-

Fifths Compromise. This compromise provision has not failed in its intent. It has exceeded its limits, and now affects all who graciously come to our shores.

In this chapter, we will focus on the dreadful economic and legal side effects the Three-Fifths Compromise agreement continues to have on our nation. Americans are being deceived and betrayed by this compromise provision, which must be exposed and analyzed. This analysis will allow us to elect future leaders who have concrete goals for re-establishing the basic principles of liberty.

Re-establishing these principles will create an economic and cultural bond between the people and their government. These actions will reshape our ideas for a fair and balanced society. Generally speaking, True Conservatism is not always opposed to change or reform, but stresses the viewpoint that it is better for society to change gradually and avoid all extremes.

> *The most important single central fact about a free market is that no exchange takes place unless both parties benefit."*
>
> **Milton Friedman**

The purpose of this chapter is not to place guilt upon any one person or ethnic group, nor is it to whine about our nation's past mistakes. We want Americans to see our nation's problems as they really exist, and to investigate different processes for their corrections. These corrections are crucial to the success and prosperity of each and every American.

To begin the process of correcting and restoring our nation's wealth we must have a common goal, where race is not the main issue. The key question should be, how can we end the victimization of the Three-Fifths Compromise upon the American people?

This compromise provision is the actual enemy of the theory of True Conservatism. It is a by-product of indecisiveness, which has led to the divisiveness of this defective act. The Founding Fathers were uncertain about the constitutionality regarding the sale of human beings as commodities.

Because of their indecisiveness on the trafficking of humans, the very existence of this Union was compromised, making it economically and culturally unbalanced. The insertion of the Three-Fifths Compromise caused the split within the Union, and is one of several reasons for reverse discrimination and the Civil War.

The Knowledge to Lead

The Founding Fathers were undoubtedly among some of the cleverest men on earth. I believe, beyond a shadow of a doubt, they would have been more than a match for the Greek philosophers. They were experts at arguing and debating legal theories. Their chief debate in 1787 was how to keep the individual states together without any state losing economically.

They were faced with a conundrum, how to form a union while at the same time regulate the importation of slaves. It was James Madison's extraordinary plan, to constitutionally compromise on the issue of slavery, that got the lawmakers attention. He had designed the language of the compromise provision to make this country appear to be anti-slavery.

When the Founders finally decided to consider the slavery issue, they agreed with James Madison's controversial plan and inserted the compromise provision into the Constitution. It was their hope that this compromise would unite a nation, without alarming the population of its future destructive outcomes. The legal theory behind the design of the Three-Fifths Compromise provision was based on the status quo's cultural belief. They believed in the supremacy of the cultural common knowledge approach to governing. They also commenced to make unconstitutional laws to promote the false idea, that all people are not born equal.

We must not allow our political leaders to continue to utilize the supremacy of the cultural common knowledge belief as if it is a constitutional mandate. Today's politicians willfully use the illusion of race to shift our attention from their primary pursuit of this nation's wealth. Race, in and of itself, is an illusion. The side effects of this illusion are the continued animosity between the status quo's cultural beliefs, and the raping of our civil liberties.

The Three-Fifths Compromise is a deception and should be viewed as a wolf in sheep's clothing, with us, the citizens, being the prey. Secretly, the language of this compromise is like ravenous wolves, economically devastating the future wealth of Americans. Few Americans are aware of the economic damage being caused by the Three-Fifths Compromise agreement. Indeed, nothing in the United States is more widespread, or more economically devastating, than our ignorance of this concealed flaw.

How does the Three-Fifths Compromise agreement affect our nation's economy? How can we, as a nation, deal with this flawed passage without going into a panic? Most of our nation's psychological, cultural and economic difficulties have originated from the Three-Fifths Compromise agreement.

Counting People as Commodities

This deceptive compromise allows for the unfairness and lack of equality to a particular segment of the population. This compromise permitted the counting of persons, who were deemed commodities, as three-fifths of their total population. This illegal process of counting three-fifths of the African population, for representation and taxation purposes, began with the census of 1790. Presently, this compromise provision denies the process of intergenerational transfer of wealth to millions of Americans.

This compromise provision has forced approximately 39.8% of the American population into some form of government welfare programs. These include Federal and State disability and unemployment programs without any definitive means for improving their condition.

The Three-Fifths Compromise agreement is also having a negative economic effect on the middle class and those in the lower economic status. We will illustrate how both the Republican and the Democratic parties are playing the race card for political gain. The illusion of race and cultural animosity will forever be a part of this nation's psyche. Every ethnic group comes to the table with their own pre-conceived notions, or impressions, about other ethnic groups.

Most religions of the world view cultural diversity as a tool with which to unite humanity. Today's political leaders utilize the supremacy of a cultural common knowledge belief as a tool to divide humanity. Presently, the cultural mindset of the

> If the American dream is for Americans only, it will remain our dreams and never be our destiny."
>
> **Rene Williamson**

status quo is projecting fear and animosity between ethnic groups. These negative projections have become a political platform for the acts of cultural violence that are divisive and explosive.

The time has come for Americans to choose the fashion in which we will debate our nation's cultural issues. We should no longer leave the issue of cultural tension in the hands of our politicians who are politically motivated to project fear. As citizens, we must accept the fact that cultural animosity is, and has always been, a normal part of our existence, our Founding Fathers understood that fact.

As a nation; we cannot allow our politicians to continue to use the illusion of race as their hidden agenda to score political points. The status quo (politicians, Wall Street and corporations) utilize the illusion of race as a blunt political tool to remain in their political positions, as well as to keep their wealth. How can we as citizens, put an end to the leadership void in Congress?

We must begin by taking advantage of the social and economic provisions that are already contained within the Constitution. These social and economic provisions are based on the theories of True Conservatism. This idea of True Conservatism was utilized in our Constitu-

> *Research has consistently shown that politicians who are successful tend to make decisions based on their constituents and are slow to reverse that well thought out position"*

tion's conception and it does not belong to any one political party or ethnic group, for it is the sum of all humanity.

Our Constitution and its method for governing, is a victory of the intellect that has been considered by many historians to be an unexpected epiphany, an intuitive leap of faith, and an understanding of a people. Many have said that an achievement such as the United States Constitution has only been accomplished twice in the history of humanity: The Old Testament of Israel and the Golden Age of Greece.

> *"True patriotism springs from a belief in the dignity of the individual, freedom and equality not only for Americans but for all people on earth."*
>
> **Eleanor Roosevelt**

The Vision of Conservatism Theories

The theory of True Conservatism is both pro-State and in favor of a small and effective government. Our government is a reflection of its people, though it is not perfect; we as Americans must thrive for its perfection. There are many problems facing us today, some of which are poverty, animosity and cultural hostility. These problems, that we are facing today, are the side-effects of the Three-Fifths Compromise agreement. This compromise agreement is a major blunder within our Constitutional rule of law.

Many of our social and cultural problems are presently being driven by the illusion of race. This illusion of race is also a by-product of the Three-Fifths Compromise agreement. This illusion of race and the Three-Fifths Compromise are one and the same.

When this compromise provision was enacted, it permitted the existence of inequality and reverse discrimination to materialize. This compromise does not only affect the rule of law, it also makes the workplace culturally unbalanced. It is a deception, as well as a betrayal, to the theory of True Conservatism.

The fundamental principles of our Constitution were modified when those in authority included this compromise provision into this document. This chapter will permit everyone to see for one's self that the compromise provision is the vehicle that reversed the true course and purpose behind the constitutional design.

The compromise provision is neither a law nor an amendment. It is the basis of the supremacy of a cultural mind set of men who used words of illusion. This compromise was written with the pretense of uniting a nation. They knew it to be unethical and unconstitutional, but they needed the Constitution to be ratified.

The Three-Fifths Compromise agreement will be revealed throughout this book to be an element of distortion. Its reckless language was inserted within the framing of the Constitution.

This made Paragraph 3, Section 2 within Article I a fundamentally flawed passage. This error in judgment has dishonored, as well as distorted, the original fundamental principles within the concept of True Conservatism.

Two wars were fought on American soil, one for liberty and the other for True Conservatism. The first was the War for Independence from Great Britain. The second, the Civil War, was a cultural battle fought over the fundamental aspects of True Conservatism. This second war devastated our nation both economically and emotionally. It was perhaps the most personal of any wars ever fought in our history.

This conflict split many American families, pitting brothers against brothers, friends against friends and ethnic groups against ethnic groups. Before this remarkable nation can become that more perfect Union, we must come to respect both sides of the conflict. It was through the pains of slavery and the indecisiveness of our lawmakers over the selling of Africans as human commodities, that lead up to the Civil War

Americans with a single voice must join forces to defeat our oldest and most menacing of foes, the Three-Fifths Compromise. This compromise provision has a hidden agenda, it is the true enemy to our Republican democracy. However, we can and we will defeat this enemy, one amendment at a time.

The Promise of Future Liberties

Both political parties in their rush for power and wealth, have hijacked our system of laws and have altered the principle ideas of our Constitution. Because of the Three-Fifths Compromise, we judge men and women by the color of their

> "The patriots are those who love America enough to see her as a model for mankind."
>
> **Adlai Stevenson**

skin, their wealth, and their political positions. Today's political parties continually ignore our country's past and the sacrifices that have been made for the promise of future liberties

The purpose of this chapter is to promote the will of the people. It is about our freedom and our desire for prosperity and economic wellness for us and for others. It is essential that we join together to formulate strategies through sound reasoning, with a focus on protecting our civil liberties and our nation's wealth. We will explore many methods by which we can control our financial futures. Allowing Congress and Wall-Street to continue making our financial decisions has proven to be a recipe for disaster.

Americans need to be aware that Washington will accomplish nothing unless we exercise our constitutional duty of dissent. This can be done without projecting fear or hatred. We must collectively get involved in the changes that are required, using the existing laws that provide for our security. We must also teach our children how to use the economic tools provided by the Constitution for their business success, as well as, to lobby or petition for change.

The majority of people born in the United States, regardless of their ethnicity, feel that they are entitled to be prosperous without any need for responsibility or sacrifice. This method of thinking can only promote hopelessness within this country. Our responsibilities to our country and our country's responsibilities to us are vital to our nation's economic success.

The Business of Running a Nation

Most Americans do not realize that our government is in the business of running a nation and, like any other business, it requires money from its citizens to function properly. The Federal Government of the United States of America was designed to operate as a non-for-profit corporation with limited amounts of capital. Just as in any large corporation, there will be business errors.

The articles of our Constitution are the articles of incorporation for our Federal Government, while the constitutional amendments are it's by laws. There are three branches to our Federal Government. The Executive Branch, where the U.S. President is comparable to the C.E.O. of a large corporation. The Legislative Branch, where Congress is comparable to the C.F.O. or treasurer. And the Judicial Branch, where the Supreme Court oversees and acts as the secretary, to insures the Executive and the Legislative branches follow the by-laws of this nation. The responsibilities of all three branches are to insure that the States function constitutionally.

Every American, regardless of what form of taxes they pay, is a co-owner and stockholder of this federal, non-profit corporation. Each Citizen of the United States has a vested interest in this corporation. As stockholders, we are entitled from our Federal Government the guarantee of liberty.

Our Constitution does not guarantee personal wealth or prosperity. However, it does guarantee the pursuit of happiness and the process for achieving economic wellness. Although the lawmakers who are responsible for managing this *Corporation /Federal Government* have been catering to the needs of Wall Street to the detriment of its *stockholders*.

The economic tools, employed by the status quo, are also available to ninety-five percent of the population. What is the advantage in complaining about Wall Street when citizens fail to learn, or apply, these economic tools for themselves.

There are some Americans who seem to think they are entitled to prosperity, without making any kind of sacrifice. It is imperative that we teach our children to take economic advantage of their constitutional privileges and to attend to their civil rights in a businesslike manner. This will bring about an economic balance between the citizens, Wall Street, and our Federal Government.

As board members of this federal non-profit corporation, it is our constitutional duty to initiate these economic changes. We can accomplish these economic changes by compelling both political parties to govern from the center, doing this will make available opportunities for success and prosperity for all citizens.

Celebrating America's Past

With the insertion of the Three-Fifths Compromise agreement, our previous lawmakers have created a vast economic and cultural crisis, which is economically affecting most Americans presently. We should not attempt to whitewash America's past if we want true economic opportunities for every American. Every country has their fair share of flawed legislation and their acknowledgement of these errors is the first step in their correction. We should celebrate America's history by accepting not only the pleasant, but also the unpleasant. America's greatness comes from her people's contributions, their energy, and their optimism.

The true heart and soul of a nation is revealed to the world by how it treats its people. We have much more to be proud of in this country than we have to be ashamed. Though for many, this compromise provision is a cruel and intolerable internal struggle for basic liberties.

This compromise provision hinders the opportunity for economic success for most Americans, it is divisive and explosive. The foundational language of the compromise provision was interwoven into the Constitution's rule of law. It is a hidden agenda which allows for five percent of the population to unlawfully control ninety- five percent of the people's power and wealth.

The fact of the matter is that denying and evading our past history has made it almost impossible for us to understand or appreciate our American culture. Our system of laws are not designed to insure that every ethnic group, regardless of their cultural beliefs, has the opportunity to become skilled in the methods for saving and transferring wealth to their families.

Our nation consists of many ethnic groups from around the world. Most, if not all, languages of the world are spoken here. As Americans, we are the most culturally and socially diverse people in the world. Because of this diversity we are at times, divided. Yet we have more common experiences than most people realize.

However, to experience the best that America has to offer, its citizens must first appreciate the value and the perspective behind the theories of True Conservatism. These theories are the cornerstones to the American economic way of life. The mindset behind these theories of True Conservatism is not about patriotism, it is about those who are grateful for our constitutional way of life. Though it is very important to understand, and to appreciate, what makes a true patriot.

Most Inspiring Patriots

A true patriot is a person that courageously contributes to his or her country, even under the most trying of circumstances. A patriot is a person whose behavior respects the culture of others and who also demands more from himself or herself than is constitutionally expected. A patriot is someone who defines adversity by doing what he or she believes to be right in spite of their fear of what other people may think.

This nation continues to prosper on the backs of these true American patriots. This includes the service men and women who have given, and continue to give, their lives for our country. Today, the most inspiring patriots I have met are the doctors, police officers, firefighters, school teachers, hospitals volunteers, as well as those parents, who teach their children about the fundamentals of loyalty to their families and their country.

These patriots have one thing in common, they have a deep and inspired love for their country and for the passionate ideals of True Conservatism. Also they feel a cultural responsibility to protect their fellow citizens. As citizens, we must not allow ourselves to continually be drawn into the destructive battle of blaming others for past injustices, without the means to resolve them collectively.

We Have Lost Our Vision

The theories of True Conservatism and the Constitution's rule of law are under siege by both political parties. These politicians have lost their vision for service to the American people, and have forgotten their constitutional duties to the states. Our legislator's have sworn an oath to uphold the Constitution's rule of law and to be accountable in their service to the people. Instead, politicians from both political parties continue to promote and protect the status quo, leaving ninety- five percent of their constituencies to fend for themselves.

Both political parties are now engaged in a feud for the domination of America's internal authority. Their main weapon of choice for maintaining this authority is pitting ethnic groups against ethnic groups. This process of *againstness* employed by the status quo is creating animosity between ethnic groups. It is this process of *againstness* that has changed the fundamental principles of our Constitution. Racial polarization and cultural profiling have diminished our aspirations for true liberty. It has created an environment that is hostile, where animosity and cultural hostilities between people of different ethnic groups are inevitable.

Each political party, in its haste for political positioning, have abandoned the theory of True Conservatism. Presently, the majority of our lawmakers believe this visionary theory to be defective and out of date. It is not the theory of True Conservatism that is defective. It is the unsound language within the Three-Fifths Compromise provision that is causing the economic disparity in America.

In The Name of Justice

When we started our research for this book, it brought to mind some of our country's most cherished moments. It also brought to mind some of our nation's past errors in judgment. However, it is these teachable moments and cherished memories that have assured us of a better way of life. As an American of African descent, it is not my desire to offend or criticize anyone because of what happened to my ancestors. These past errors were done in the name of what was thought to be justice, I certainly do not blame God.

I've learned by experience that my ancestor's enslavement and struggles facilitated the formation of this nation. They labored and perished due to the hostile environment of slavery. This made the cost of my freedom, as an American, worth the hardship of slavery itself.

As Americans, we should never forget, it was also a painful experience for those who fought and died in the Revolutionary War, as well as, those who fought and died in the Civil War. As an American of African descent, I am proud of this Union, along with the tremendous contributions of the Confederacy. Because of slavery's past, the Revolutionary War and the Civil War, we have established a prosperous nation.

It was this process of my ancestor's anticipation

> *His fore parents came to America in immigration ships. My foreparents came to America in slave ships. But whatever the original ships, we're in the same boat tonight*
>
> **Rev. Jessie Jackson**

for liberty that allowed me to become an American. It was also this process of my ancestor's enslavement, and their anticipation of independence for their descendents, that is now part of this nation's fortune

I have learned that being an American is not just a state of mind, or a name on a driver's license. One also has the constitutional responsibility to economically assist the Union. Therefore, as an American of African descent, I will do my best to chart my own course in life, just as all Americans should. We need to understand that regardless of our ethnicity, we are the guardians of our Constitution. That is why, it is imperative that leadership be demanded from both political parties as well as the citizens.

Who's Dominating Our Society?

There are members from both political parties who believe that True Conservatism would lead to the domination of our society. It is also believed that True Conservatism is a destructive system of inequalities and prejudices founded on deception, and that it has no useful purpose within our Republican/ Democracy. Both political parties have the audacity to call themselves patriots, while rejecting the theory of True Conservatism.

Modern liberals theorize that Republicans/Conservatives use social and cultural issues to create animosity and cultural hostility among ethnic groups for personal gain. Liberals also use the same social and cultural issues as a way to mask their own economic objectives. These hypocritical acts by both political parties hurt not only the people in opposition, but also the people within their party.

The fundamental goal of the theory of True Conservatism was to establish a form of liberty that would endure any issue of dissent. Most liberals continue to believe that the main goal of True Conservatism is to pass positions of privilege and wealth to their children. If this is true, then all Americans should be focusing on passing wealth and constitutional responsibility to their descendents, as well.

In this chapter we have outlined the pros and cons of the theory of True Conservatism. This theory has not changed much throughout this nation's history. Presently, the theory of True Conservatism seems to be unfamiliar to many Americans. This unfamiliarity is not a recent phenomenon, even to those individuals who claim to be Conservatives.

Political Correctness

Today's policies of "political correctness," have become a search-and-destroy campaign of any evidence of integrity within Washington. In our opinion, the flamboyant rhetoric of people such as Rush Limbaugh, Ann Coulter or Michael Moore, is representative of what is good about a Republican/Democracy. It allows for freedom of speech and gives citizens the constitutional right to voice their opinion on how our government should function.

Next, we'll take a look at how some Liberals in Congress think they are superior to Conservatives at overhauling existing federal programs. These so-called methods of reforms by Liberals are stereotypical, since both political parties are using flawed messages of projections to win votes.

These stereotypical words of projection, which produce fear among ethnic groups, are powerful tools used by both party's strategists to manufacture outrage in Americans. We caught a glimpse of that outrage in the summer of 2009 over the issues of heath care. It is important that citizens have a thorough understanding of the Constitution's birth and its history. Citizens need to utilize their constitutional privileges in a business like fashion and be able to perceive when they are being violated. We must also be constitutionally prepared to defend our fellow Americans.

Most of us are convinced that politicians in Washington D. C. are more interested in their re- election than in our well-being. Although, it is our responsibility, as citizens, to debate the imperfections of our system of laws and make judgments as to their merits for change or removal. We must remember that we have the advantage of experience on our side, unlike the Framers of the Constitution. They were neither more inspired, wiser, or in greater possession of integrity then we are today. Though we should honor and appreciate their accomplishments.

However, presently our politicians have lost their focus and it is our responsibility to help them return to the fundamental principles of True Conservatism. The freedoms that we enjoy are the results of our ancestor's hard work. They committed themselves to the writing of the Constitution to pull together a raw nation. We must make every effort to keep this living and timeless document evolving, just as the people of this country have evolved.

We should begin serious and honest debates on our nation's constitutional wrongs. Once these truths are articulated, the issues cannot be glossed over or ignored. There are some in this country who do not want to hear or speak the truth. Then there are some politicians who are devoted to the truth, even when it is political suicide. For lawmakers and citizens to remain silent while others are being economically harmed, breeds contempt..

With truth comes change and change is inevitable, if truth is to prevail. Lawmakers know what needs to be said and what has to be done to correct these cultural and economic issues. However, their fear of change, along with their fear of losing their political positions, prevent them from upholding their oath of office. Each member of Congress has sworn to serve both their state and their constituents.

Therefore, as citizens, we must open our eyes and stop our self-destructive role of ignorance. We must demand that those in Congress uphold their oath of office and put the needs of their constituent's first. If not, they should be promptly removed from office. Many constitutional amendments that would have benefitted citizens were sabotaged by both political parties. This was done to preserve a false sense of peace in this country, while many of our cultural and economic issues were being glossed over.

Politicians are not willing to make any serious attempts to resolve these issues. These amendments would relieve cultural tensions and the economic disparity within our nation. We are residing in a nation with an underlying false hope of peace, making life for many unbearable. This creates a reckless and an unpleasant environment, where unsupported information can thrive.

In the final analysis, Americans appreciate frankness more than a cover-up. As a people, we must care enough to confront and resolve our cultural and economic issues collectively. If not, we cannot cultivate or encourage others to dream of an ideal Union. We need the courage to speak up before it is too late.

The Thoughtless Actions of People

Frankness is not a license, nor is it a right, to speak whenever, wherever, or whatever you want. There is a time and a place to properly debate every issue. The thoughtless actions of people who debate the illusion of race, using unsympathetic vocabulary, are lacking in integrity.

These thoughtless actions destroy the lives of people and leave lasting wounds, which hinder any future debates. We must, through the use of proactive discussions, have

> *We have lived our entire lives in this country without a blueprint for national sanity*
>
> **Bill Gates**
> **author, age 53**

the courage to confront the economic and psychological crisis's brought on by the rejection of True Conservatism.

As citizens, we are responsible for the actions of our elected officials. Arrogance and stubborn pride between ethnic groups and our political leaders will quickly destroy solidarity among citizens. The noble language within our Constitution is the bridge that brings people together with dignity. It is very important that our lawmakers govern with humility and not with self gratification. A proactive approach to governing allows lawmakers to design legislation that will assist the average American to assimilate easier into the mainstream of society

If we, as Americans, fail to exhibit pride in our federal government, and continue to be anti- authority, we will hinder the blessings of liberty to ourselves and others who are counting on our Constitution's governing powers. The Constitution states that we "*The People*" must bear the 'burden' of being its guardian.

As guardians, when it comes to defending the constitutional sovereignty of our country, we must not fear anything or anyone. Our Founding Fathers had the foresight to create laws that would evolve with its citizens. They understood that these laws of inclusion were the fundamental keys to a successful Union. Nations that are committed to equality come into being when the people know that their opinions matter.

We have made many provocative statements in this chapter with which you can agree or disagree. Nevertheless, no one, at this point, can disagree with the fact that the Three-Fifths Compromise agreement is economically and psychologically destroying American's self worth. We cannot easily undo decades of reckless leadership over night. Though, we can prevent this compromise provision from continuing its destruction of our nation's economy and our future civil liberties

The Necessity of Taxation

Those who are working, or paying any form of taxes, are constitutionally entitled to utilize any governmental program created for the benefit of the states. Most Americans do not appreciate the fact, that their tax dollars are an investment in the Federal Government. When you invest a portion of your income in Uncle Sam, or pay for any taxable product, you have economically invested in your future, and that of your State. Even the poorest in our country pay some form of taxes. They, too, are the stockholders of this nonprofit corporation.

All civilized societies require a variety of public services. This, in turn, requires a moderate and reasonable tax to be collected from its citizens. Despite the decades of conservative and liberal rhetoric on the unfair implementation of the tax codes, the majority of Americans are still willing to pay their fair share in taxes. Yet the Liberals are constantly being clobbered by the Conservatives with their rhetoric about taxation being unfairly implemented towards the rich. It is not the liberal agenda, nor is their legislation, that is the cause of taxation being unfairly implemented. It is the language within the Three-Fifths Compromise agreement which is the culprit. This compromise provision has made it almost impossible for the commerce department to design a fair policy of taxation.

It is time for Congress to end the debates on how much will be spent on programs that economically support the middle class and the disadvantaged. Instead, the debate should be about what citizens will receive for that expenditure. Conservatives should stop implying that their tax policies are "tax cuts". What Republicans and Conservatives are actually doing is delaying taxation to the next generation. These delays in tax increases are detrimental to the economic future of Americans.

Changing Your Approach to Citizenry

We want to insure that you understand this chapter is not just about your constitutional rights. It is also about the theories of True Conservatism, and how these concepts are a pathway to economic equality within our nation. These concepts, and the fundamental principle that all men and women are created equal, are centered around the theories of True Conservatism.

The Founders were aware that God is the only one capable of governing man's morality. They also recognized that the Constitution would not possess any power to legislate morality. The Founding Fathers used the theories of True Conservatism as their guide. They understood that these theories would oppose any major change that would halt the process of equality.

As an American of African descent, I discovered that for me to become successful, and to make a difference in the lives of others, I had to learn the economic rules that governed my economic existence. Learning these constitutional rules has allowed for me to understand who I am. I am a proud citizen of the United States of America, and nothing else really matters. Therefore, to protect our civil liberties and our incomes, we must learn these constitutional business rules if we are to become economically successful in this country.

Is America's Culture Vanishing ?

As citizens, we must come to understand that for our nation to mature economically and psychologically, any discussion as to which ethnic group is morally right or wrong is futile. Our problems are far greater than the status quo's illusion of fairness. These debates should be about the survival of our American culture/*society*

We can no longer continue to allow our personalities, our backgrounds and our fears of others, to influence how we vote. Voting in this fashion is not being patriotic, it is being selfish, lazy, and ignorant of the real issues in play. Americans will go to the polls in record numbers to vote for the next U.S. president. Some voters will crave for the feeling of social stability, while others will crave for social change.

No nation of people can choose the right man or woman for the job of governing when they are voting with regard to their cultural mind set and not on the facts before them. It seems that Liberals and Conservatives are divided according to their personality and their cultural beliefs.

Presently, when a person votes in anger and does not accept the facts in front of them, it is their expression of selfishness. Most of the time voters do not have direct access to the outside world. Everything is filtered through radio, TV and the internet. For that reason, each of us creates a mental image of the world that is representative of our own point of view. This cultural mind-set is what guides each person in their perception of the government and their political candidates. These perceptions include those social features preferred or despised by each individual.

What Makes a Liberal or a Conservative?

There are certain cultural and personal characteristics that generally influence whether a person will succumb to being a liberal or a conservative. These include ethnicity, education, gender, age and a person's cultural mind-set.

> "A man should look for what is, and not for what he thinks should be."
>
> **Albert Einstein**

It has been said that most liberals view the social inequity of preferred groups as unjust and unconstitutional. They know that correcting these injustices will require reform, and that reform means opposition. The problem with any *reform, or change,* is how much and how many millions of citizens will be affected by that change?

It has also been revealed that most liberals believe in the separation of church and state. They are sometimes known as *ditheists*, as were most of the Founding Fathers. It was not because these men did not believe in a God, but they understood that God would not interfere in the affairs of man. The Founders believed in the existence of two independent powers. One perfect, which is God and the other, flawed which is man.

The Founding Fathers understood the underlying principle of man's existence. They recognized that men were being governed by two different principles. One principle is the workings of the church, which is headed by God. The other principle is our constitutional rule of law, which is governed by man. The Church is a divinely ordained institution, purposely designed to deal with moral issues only. Our Constitution's rule of laws are legal theories, purposely designed by man for legal issues. The Framers understood that these two principles must remain separate, since they have two distinct and different purposes.

This separation of church and state does not prohibit the involvement of religious believers in the areas of social and economic responsibility. Therefore, citizens who are committed to religion are also responsible for paying their fair share of taxes. They are also responsible for actively speaking out for what is constitutionally and morally dishonest. There are no honorable excuses that would justify not participating in this nation's economic development.

Presently, Liberal and Conservative thinkers have created a political division between those favoring Civil Rights and those favoring Religious Rights. This is why citizens who favor Civil liberties believe that Gay Rights should be handled by individual states. These same citizens also understand the need for some type of welfare, universal health care and women's rights.

It seems that most liberals have an ability to see solutions to complex and ambiguous social problems. The majority of liberal thinkers have become judges, social workers and professors. These are careers that require an appreciation of opposing points of view.

However, more has to be done to stem the tide of economic disparity within our nation. To establish a fair and balanced society Congress, along with Wall Street and Main Street, must pioneer a revolutionary economic plan designed to educate America's children in the art of creating wealth and saving that wealth. These economic agendas will assist the disadvantaged in the art of establishing intergenerational transfer of wealth to their next generations. The transferring of wealth, no matter how large or small, is the next generation's economic starting point.

These types of programs will be required to begin the process of erasing economic disparity in this country. These economic programs will also assist and eliminate millions of Americans from the dole/welfare and unemployment. It would only cost 1% of this nation's federal budget to refocus our efforts in assisting the unfortunate to assimilate into the middle class. This assimilation effort is necessary for this nation to economically survive

Unfortunately, it has been demonstrated throughout today's political arena that some, if not most, conservatives are willing to defend the current social inequalities. They will help the underprivileged only as necessary, or when they are forced to do so by a constitutional amendment or an executive order.

Even the Founders understood that change would be inevitable. They also knew that change would be hard, but necessary. When changes are implemented, these changes must be of benefit to all citizens, including Wall-Street and Main Street.

The United States Constitution is not a perfect document. These rules of law look good on paper, but our Constitution still requires our assistance to cultivate it into what it was meant to be. This Constitution is a set of rules written to enhance the economic lives of those who walk on our shores, regardless of their ethnically. Our system of laws cannot operate successfully until we begin to exercise the power that was given to us by the Founders.

Most Americans have the wrong impression about the role of the Federal Government and its abilities to economically assist its citizens. We are being told by the status quo that the government is our adversary, but that is far from the truth. They know that if we are always annoyed with our government we will never have time to assist in its improvement. Citizens must view the regulations of our Federal Government as economic tools designed for success and not weights around our necks. How you view your government depends on your cultural mind set.

This chapter has demonstrated, without a shadow of a doubt, that the theory of True Conservatism is the language and ideas upon which our nation was founded. This theory is the cornerstone to American way of life. True Conservatism is a celebration of our country's governing charter and the foundation upon which all generations of Americans can place their trust.

IS AN APOLOGY FOR THE THREE-FIFTHS COMPROMISE A NECESSITY?

In establishing this nation, the Founders illogically perfected a unsettling provision within the Constitution. This provision is a constitutional conspiracy. The language of this provision has permitted the policymakers to draft a revolutionary plan to take advantage of commerce and other economic resources well into the future.

This provision is called the Three-Fifths Compromise agreement. The idea behind this reckless provision was to control both the wealth and the transactions of the *people*. This compromise provision has constitutionally permitted lawmakers to conspire and oppose human rights of any ethnic group, other than their own.

The status quo utilizes the language within this provision to identify the African population as being enemies and inferior. In this way, the policymakers could rationalize the use of this compromise provision to confiscate a person's resources by constitutional authority.

The Three-Fifths Compromise has allowed policymakers to maintain their control over the very resources the victims need to economically assimilate into the main stream of society. This compromise provision is a hidden agenda that has economic and social consequences for both the oppressed and the oppressor.

Presently, most Americans are not aware of the psychological or the economic impact the Three-Fifths Compromise is having on our society as a whole. As a nation, we have tolerated this mutual adversary and, in our ignorance and self-centeredness, is permitting it to exist. This provision terminated the privilege of our constitutional rule of law for some and replaced it with the dispensing of hopelessness for millions of Americans.

The Three-Fifths Compromise is in total opposition to everything that is true and real within our nation. It is devastating our nation's financial future and, at the same time, creating poverty, ghettos, violence and political disorder. We will demonstrate that this compromise provision weakens our finances and impairs our national security.

Constitutional Apartheid

By now, you have discovered that the Three-Fifths Compromise agreement is written to validate constitutional apartheid within our system of laws. It has altered the very safeguards that are imbedded within the Constitution for the protection of the people. This is why some form of oversight is necessary to curb the abuse of those who oversee the workings of our government.

James Madison, the architect of the Three Fifths Compromise, once quoted, "If men and women were

> *Discrimination against gays is just as needless, just as hurtful, just as damaging to those it affects as all other forms of discrimination. Let's face it, there's nothing very positive about being a bigot*
>
> **Tom, a 23-year-old former journalists**

governed by guardian angels, neither external nor internal government control by men would be a necessity. In framing a government, which is to be administered by men, over men, the great difficulty lies in the fact that you must first enable that government to control the governed. While at the same time this government is obligated to control itself".

In a free society, it's the government's responsibility to protect the civil rights of individuals the same way it protects religious rights. In a society where religious rights supersede civil rights, the religious factions will readily oppress the civil rights of individuals. Without this understanding of governance, anarchy will reign as the natural state. Then the civil liberty of the individual will not be secured against the hostility of religious groups.

The language within the Three-Fifths Compromise agreement places religious rights over those of civil liberties. This compromise provision is a civil right issue, unlike slavery, which is a moral issue. Presently, our Constitution is not designed to deal with the immoral aftermath of slavery's past. Though, our Constitution does have the proper and the legal tools to deal directly with the economic and psychological impact of this compromise provision. The language of this provision is still part of the basic frame work of our Constitution, and it must be constitutionally amended.

Sanctioned and Approved by Legislators

No citizen should have to assume the economic burden of both slavery's past and the Three-Fifths Compromise agreement. Both of these fraudulent acts were sanctioned and approved by past legislators. The burden of slavery's past and the Three-Fifths Compromise are the sole responsibility of our Federal Government. It is the responsibility of present and future legislators in Congress to make constitutional corrections. It is also the responsibility of citizens to insure that our legislators address these issues proactively. With that said, we must appreciate the fact that the noble language of our Constitution's rule of law is fundamentally sound.

When our Constitution's rule of law is employed fairly, all defects within its writing's can be corrected. The insertion of the Three-Fifths Compromise agreement into the Constitution is a constitutional tragedy and should be treated as such. Therefore, a formal constitutional apology, designed as an amendment, is the only legal correction to this constitutional misdeed.

Failing to amend this compromise provision is a never ending shame of humiliation. It is economically

> *"Each generation should be made to bear the burden of its own wars, instead of carrying them on, at the expense of other generations."*
>
> **James Madison**

> *"As a man is said to have a right to his property, he may be equally said to have a property in his rights. "*
>
> **James Madison**

and emotionally appalling to its victims. Amending this compromise provision will allow us, as a nation, to move forward in re-examining the different ways of resolving our cultural and economic problems.

Americans must come to the realization that the Three-Fifths Compromise agreement is a complex interaction of theories, attitudes and actions by individuals and organizations. To continue to be a successful and prosperous nation, we must acknowledge to one another this constitutional misdeed. A constitutional apology for the Three-Fifths Compromise agreement will be the beginning of the process of restoring our nation's wealth. This apology will be a complex constitutional task to accomplish. The first step in correcting this constitutional flaw is to scrutinize the evidence of the misconduct.

Historical Misdeeds

A few years back the Protestant and the Southern Baptist churches, in their conventions in Atlanta, Georgia, initiated a process for correcting these constitutional errors. Both denominations confessed to their religious wrongdoing with regard to slavery and the compromise provision. They also prayed that their confession would be the beginning of this nation's cultural healing. These churches understood that if the country persisted in not correcting these injustices, the nation would continue to reap the bitter harvest of despair. The Atlanta delegates apologized for their failure to take action against individuals and organizations that engaged in these acts of cultural discrimination.

The remorse shown by these two churches was the latest wave of Christians to unburden their souls by repenting for their ancestors historical misdeeds. However, more must be done within our system of laws with regard to this compromise provision and not just the emancipation of one's inner self.

> *"In no instance have the churches been guardians of the liberties of the people."*
>
> **James Madison**

The holy book of any religion demonstrates that there must be more to correcting a wrong than just repentance or apologies. The commitment to repentance for past wrongs by any religion or government must always be followed by some form of restitution.

Presently, politicians are most comfortable when they are detached from the rush for restitution, because these transgressions originated within the framing of the Constitution. They know that true repentance is costly, because this form of restitution will not be cheap. Americans have become comfortable with their own detachment from the hostility and animosity within our country. This false sense of confidence causes many in this country to believe that things are becoming culturally better. This belief, or feeling, leaves us, as a nation, dysfunctional.

> *I have no doubt but that the misery of the lower classes will be found to abate whenever the Government assumes a freer aspect and the laws favor a subdivision of Property."*
>
> **James Madison**

The events in Atlanta, Georgia, by the Protestant and the Southern Baptist churches were remarkably similar to those that occurred in South Africa. The Dutch Reformed Church gathered north of Johannesburg and formally apologized to Native South Africans for engaging in its practice of religious justification for apartheid.

Unlike the Africans of South Africa; who had the international news media to communicate their plight to the world, the African population in America, during slavery, did not have the advantage of any global communications. There were no media communications such as; radio or television to show the horror the American African population had to endure. Many millions of African slaves and their descendants had to endure four hundred years of *Religious Justification* for slavery in this country. Presently, millions of Americans, regardless of the ethnicity, are dealing with the economic aftermath of slavery's past.

There are no words to articulate the inhumanity of one man's appalling treatment towards another. The continuous separation of people by color, gender, and ethnicity in this country will ultimately cause our nation to bear its second most dramatic cultural clash in its history. The first cultural clash was the Civil War.

Discussing the necessity of an apology for the Three-Fifths Compromise agreement does not resolve anything immediately, but it is a necessary first step. An official apology by the Federal Government with the endorsement of the American people, coupled with restitution, will meet the requirements of true repentance. It is our hope that this constitutional correction will give our country a true sense of brotherhood, as was felt in the new Union of South Africa.

The Dutch Reformed Church's repentance was well thought-out and sincere, and there was some form of restitution for its victims. However, are the apologies from the American Baptist and Protestant churches sincere? As authors, we feel that the apologies from these churches are heartfelt. However, for the apologies to be effective, restitution must follow repentance! Despite this fact, restitution has not yet been paid, or even debated, among those in Congress or by religious leaders.

The Afrikaners had more in their favor because they apologized for their religious apartheid while their country was in the grip of a violent transition. The Southern Baptist Convention offered their apology one hundred and sixty years after slavery. Consider the economic effects of an apology when our government apologizes and establishes a federal program of restitution.

Acknowledgment of Responsibility

The Three-Fifths Compromise agreement is the primary source of our present day cultural hostilities. Our institutions and neighborhoods are boiling over with ethnic animosities. They are in disarray and have developed into breeding grounds of deadly, cultural confrontations.

Americans have the responsibility, and the obligation, to assist in the process of restoring our country's wealth and nobility. This process of a Constitutional apology will help to re-establish the fundamental principles of True Conservatism. In addition, the victims of this compromise experience must also realize that they too have an economic and cultural responsibility in the restitution process. Their heartfelt forgiveness for our nation's past injustices is just as important as an apology for that past.

Unlike most history books, that only focus on the moral effects of slavery, this book deals with the legal and economic side-effects of the Three-Fifths Compromise agreement, the Civil War and Slavery's past. This compromise provision is equivalent to a form of economic and legal enslavement. As a nation, we must come to realize how this intolerable compromise provision has affected us. We must find legal and proactive methods to correct these constitutional wrongs.

There is a collective feeling of shame among the descendants of American slave owners. While among African Americans there is a feeling of both shame and economic despair. Both descendants bear some form of stigma from the slavery experience. Though presently, we are all experiencing the dreadful economic scam of the Three-Fifths Compromise agreement.

There are those well-intentioned Americans who say that slavery was only a small part of American history. They wonder why Americans of African descent cannot get over the pains of slavery and move on. These responses and well intentioned replies are real, and may sound noble to some, but does nothing to resolve the economic affliction of slavery's past.

Since Congress refuses to debate the issue of paying any form of reparation to the descendents of former slaves, the victims must constitutionally take matters into their own hands. There has been considerable dialogue among some Americans of African descent with regard to financial compensation for the two million acres of land that was unconstitutionally confiscated by democratic President Andrew Johnson in 1865. These conversations follow the legal procedures that were successfully used by Americans of Japanese descent. Their lands were also confiscated by the United States Government at the beginning of World War II.

Congress must make the same legal procedures available to Americans of African descent as those afforded to Americans of Japanese descent. Although, money has never been the main issue for Americans of African descent. There is little that can compensate these Americans for their loss, or the permanent altering, of their history and their heritage.

Giving Americans of African descent a choice between receiving a government handout or full acknowledgment for the government's past offenses, we believe the majority would choose the latter. The psychological impact of a sincere apology would have a greater economic influence than whatever monies the government might see fit to disburse to the descendants of American slaves.

More importantly, the majority of African Americans must understand that they too have a responsibility in this healing process. The process of a constitutional apology will be the first step in establishing the faith that African American's should have in the principles of True Conservatism. We must bear in mind that the decisions we allow our government to make are a fundamental part of democracy. If we permit our policymakers to continue to make unethical choices, it is we who are to blame.

We know that our Constitution allows for new amendments. The Framers created the tools within the Constitution to make amendments, when necessary. These adjustments are never painless. Amending the Three-Fifths Compromise is a necessity for the economic survival of our Union. The fundamentals of the conservatism theory of equality are one of our many constitutional privileges, which permit us to dissent and challenge our politicians.

> *Democracy is worth dying for, because it's the most deeply honorable form of government ever devised by man.*
>
> **Ronald Reagan**

The Stolen Generations

Whatever you have accomplished in your life, and whatever your values are, everyone within this nation is bound by this unproductive compromise provision. We have many challenges in this country, but our most pressing challenge should be amending this dreadful Three-Fifths Compromise agreement.

Our nation will continue to pay a high price for its failure to amend this compromise provision and invest in education and job creation. Politicians purposely failed to invest in the underprivileged and because of this, one child out of four will be living in some form of poverty. We must discover methods that will keep our young people in schools instead of sending them off to prisons.

These methods will insure that our standard of living does not continue to drop, thereby forcing more families into ghettos. Investing economically into these communities will allow the disadvantaged to assimilate more easily into main stream society. This will, in turn, help create more tax revenues.

The majority of Americans have conveniently forgotten how the Federal Government, in the past, designed programs that allowed European immigrants, within ghettos, to assimilate and become middle class citizens. Today, ghettos have become disconnected entities within this country. They have developed into economic prisons, where whole communities economically have to depend solely on the welfare system.

Escaping the Ghetto's Grip

The status quo views ghettos as isolated areas of poorly educated, low income or destitute Americans. It is these Americans who are economically being preyed upon by the fraudulent language within the compromise provision. These ghettos have become government supported outposts that are purposely designed to halt the assimilation of people into main stream society. The status quo uses the welfare system, not as a pathway to assimilation, but as a tool to keep people trapped within these communities.

> *During the last 30 years the number of children living in poverty has increased by nearly 30 percent with the greatest increase among white kids."*
>
> **Vanishing Dreams.**

That is why a good number of Americans within ghettos have attained, and have acquired, a highly observant wisdom. This wisdom is a rare perspective, or outlook, on one's life that cannot be shared by the status quo. People who live in ghettos are exposed everyday to the feelings and experiences of economic despair.

For most of these Americans, the dream for economic wellness is either a pipe dream or a nightmare that causes many to forever lose the hope of living a normal life. Ghettos are basic way stations used by the status quo. These ghettos have been covertly transformed into places of economic enslavement. Our lawmakers and corporations are making huge profits off the poor and deprived within these ghettos.

Every day there are millions of children growing up without any choices for education, jobs or even the prospect of escaping the ghetto's grip. Mary Goodman is a good example of how poverty-stricken people, who live in ghettos, daily, exist on the edge of economic violence. Mary was born in1974 in a dilapidated hospital in Gary, Indiana. The doctor discharged Mary and her single mother from the hospital and they were sent home to a public housing project. Sirens, screams and gunshots were constantly the background noises of Mary's difficult life.

Violence and brutality and being hungry were a reality for Mary, who as a child always reminded her younger brother to watch his back every day when she left for school. There were times that she would not play outside for fear that she might be shot. Everyone she knew had been affected by some sort of gun violence or was living in some form of property.

Mary is fourteen, in the seventh grade, and has always attended the school in her deprived neighborhood. The educational system within her community continues to fail her. She is reading at the fourth grade level and has no understanding of long division. Her teachers are afraid to hold her back. They believe that it would not make any difference.

> *In the last 10 years, the number of functionally illiterate 17 years and older has more than doubled. Today, 7 million teenagers are functionally illiterate.*
>
> **Children's Defense fund**

Mary has been recently raped, stabbed in the arm and robbed at a public park while walking home from school. Though the doctors were able to sew up her punctured arm, they were unable to surgically remove her fear of society as a whole. She will be very lucky if she reaches the age of eighteen without going to prison. There are millions of young Mary's in these ghettos, who are living life on the edge of violence without any economic hope.

We live in the wealthiest of countries, and yet we have inner-city ghettos and poor rural areas throughout the nation growing at an alarming rate. Year after year millions of children, like Mary, are born into this same situation and nothing seems to change for them.

Taxpayers continue to pay the tab for unemployment benefits, food stamps, hospital bills and prisons. Mary may end up going to prison for a crime that she may have committed against you, or your family. But, the only real crime that was committed here was committed against Mary, by the status quo. Mary is a bright, young girl. Her legacy is that she was born an American citizen of European descent, in an underprivileged family, living in the ghettos. She and her family are also victims of the boomerang effects of The Three-Fifths Compromise agreement

Most Americans have not comprehended the economic and psychological damage this compromise provision has had on them and their descendents. This compromise, as intended, has not failed in its design. It has over- reached it purpose and is now affecting all those who have freely come to these shores.

However, the methods used in the Americanization of the African population were violent, unconstitutional, and beyond man's understanding. Because of the inhumane treatment of the African population, the victims and their descendents were deprived of their traditional cultures, family names, social organizations and their human rights.

This population for over two hundred years has been constitutionally labeled commodities or three fifths of a population. Presently, the descendents of American African slaves are the only ethnic group that did not enter this country looking for a better way of life. They were people transported to this country from Africa, by slave traders. The act of transporting people to another country for the express purpose of free labor was endorsed by the Federal Government. These bureaucrats stood to make millions of dollars off human trafficking.

> *Knowledge will forever govern ignorance; and a people who mean to be their own governors must arm themselves with the power which knowledge gives."*
>
> **James Madison**

The African slave population was forced to work for the status quo and was constitutionally regarded as the property of the slave owner. The only assimilation process available to Americans of African descent was, and still is, founded on the key elements of the Three-Fifths Compromise experience.

This compromise provision is the corruption of the traditions and the identities of Americans of African descent. This particular ethnic group was being sold as a commodity and stamped with slave names like Bill Gates and Robert Gates. How can a nation place a price tag on an ethnic group's lost humanity and stolen income? As an author of this book, as well as a descendant of African slaves, I have asked myself this very same question for the better part of my life.

In the past, as new immigrants became Americanized, they were entitled to take advantage of a constitutional entitlement known as *assimilation or upper mobility*. This allows newcomers to blend into main stream society and eventually into Wall-Street. This ability of assimilation is what makes America great. It is this process of assimilation and integration which affords immigrants their Due Process. This process, coupled with hard work, allows most Americans to become economically sound. Therefore, as naturalized citizens, they were entitled to benefit from any economic program designed by Congress.

This assimilation aided the European immigrant with their new life in America. It was this assimilation and integration that gave them the economic tools to become economically productive. The African population in America, and their descendants, were constitutionally denied the right to assimilate into main stream society, unlike other ethnic groups.

Because of the Three-Fifths-Compromise agreement, Congress disregarded the human rights of people brought from Africa. It was deemed these Africans were not immigrants looking for a better life. They were legally

> "The essence of Government is power; and power, lodged as it must be in human hands, will ever be liable to abuse."
>
> **James Madison**

labeled, within the Constitution, as felons and commodities to be bought and sold to the highest bidder.

Since the African population was legally labeled as property, they were not entitled to any constitutional entitlements. The 13th, 14th and15th amendments failed to constitutionally correct the economic and psychological damage caused by the Three-Fifths Compromise agreement. The purposes of these three amendments were not to correct the negative effect of this compromise provision, but were designed to end the physical side of slavery.

It is almost impossible for Americans of African descent to incorporate into main stream society, without the process of genuine assimilation. No other ethnic group within this nation has ever had to endure the wrath of a constitutional purging

The Assimilation Process

The cultural and economic foundation for Americans of African descent is not based on integration or assimilation. It is surviving the hardships related to the hollow promises of the Emancipation Act and the fraudulent language within the Three-Fifths Compromise agreement.

The assimilation process was constitutionally forbidden to Americans of African descent, they largely ended up living in ghettos without the economic means for escape. Previously, ghettos were places for the process of assimilation to materialize for Jews, Irish, Italians and other immigrants.

Ghettos now serve as places of mistrust, because politicians purposely fail to fully incorporate disadvantaged people into the main stream of *their society*. As for the fraudulent language

> *Wherever there is interest and power to do wrong, wrong will generally be done."*
>
> **James Madison**

of the Three-Fifths Compromise agreement, there is a sense of hopelessness and a lack of political interest among those living within these ghettos.

Americans of African descent are the only ethnic group within this country who have constitutionally suffered systematically, both in the past and in the present, from the exclusion and discrimination based on the experiences of slavery and the Three-Fifths Compromise fiasco. This population lives with the uncertainty that one day they will be totally free from this constitutional misdeed.

Legal Action Against the Compromise Provision

The sinister language of the Three-Fifths Compromise agreement is ingrained into the text of our Constitution. It has infected our national spirit to the point that the middle class has become this nation's new form of slavery. As authors, we feel that a constitutional apology for The Three-Fifths Compromise would, in effect, be an act of courage and patriotism.

As stated earlier, the Three-Fifths Compromise agreement and the slavery experience are two separate issues. Slavery, in itself, is a moral and insufferable issue, which will be dealt with by God. That's why our lawmakers are not concerned about paying reparations/compensation for the acts of slavery. They too deem that the act of slavery is in God's hands. Could they be right in their assumption? The word "slavery" was never introduced into the language of the Constitution and therefore is not deemed to be a legal matter. Americans must come to the realization that our Constitution was purposely designed to deal with legal issues only.

The insertion of this compromise provision is a binding constitutional contract with the states. This compromise provision was the means used by past legislators to keep the word "slavery" from appearing within the Constitution. It was the policymaker's method of concealing the government's legal responsibility for the crime of permitting the sale of human beings as commodities.

The majority of Americans of African descent expect some form of reparation for the economic impairment caused by the slavery experience. Though, as we said earlier, slavery itself is a moral issue. Therefore, reparation from the government for the immorality of slavery cannot be had at this time.

The process of reparation is not the only legal channel for the redressing of past injustices. Clearly, the laws for Restitution and Retribution are the constitutional channels that will address and correct this compromise provision head-on. Congress has a constitutional obligation to debate the issues of compensation by restitution for the fraudulent act of this compromise provision.

The act of restitution is a constitutional law of gain-based recovery, or repayment from the victimizers. While retribution is, by contrast, the constitutional law of justice, or recovery, for the victims. This will not only have an overwhelming impact on the restoration of our nation's wealth, but on the victim's economic status as well. It will be an economic, psychological and motivational transformation for the American people.

We will make a case that legal action against this compromise provision is a necessity. Amending this compromise provision, will not only boost the collective psyche of Americans, but would promote a major decrease in many of our nation's social and economic problems. Congress has a constitutional duty to guarantee that no person shall be deprived of their property, their liberty, or their Due Process under the law.

The Three-Fifths Compromise agreement is a victimizer. It is the responsibility of Congress to right the wrongs of past congressional sessions. Most politicians refuse, or are unable to recognize, the distasteful fact that this compromise provision is a fraudulent constitutional act.

The truth is many in this country persist on being narrow-minded on this issue. Our policymakers are continuing to conceal this compromise provision by the most sophisticated, subtle and indirect forms of congressional rulings.

The Practices of Exclusion and Rejection

In this country, a person's cultural beliefs, their ethnicity and their skin color, is the single most notable split within our laws. Our economy and our social infrastructures are both controlled by the effects of the compromise provision. Our national consciousness and the various processes and practices of exclusion, rejection and the subjection of a people by this compromise provision, is built into our major public institutions.

Americans of European and African descent have fought great wars against dictatorships that had, at their core, the destruction of freedom for all humanity. They each fought against practiced genocide. Americans of African descent have fought and died in these wars, so that other ethnic groups from around the world could gain their freedom. Though they themselves have not been set free from the lethal grip of the Three-Fifths Compromise agreement.

This nation needs to take a hard look at the degree to which the act of this compromise slaughtered the language and the heritage of African Americans. The language within this compromise provision is also the vehicle which allows some groups in this country to vilify the South, as if the South is responsible for today's economic calamity.

Currently, society celebrates Black History month, where politicians issue proclamations and pay tribute to notable Americans of African descent. Although, as soon as February ends, it's back to business as usual, no hope, no assimilation, and no economic ability to empower themselves.

The Thin Line Between Fact and Fantasy

As a whole, America has failed to reveal how African Americans ideas and inventions have enriched the lives of many

Americans. Most of our institutions have played a large part in the omission of African American history, systematically removing it from history books. Many history books fail to admit that Americans of African descent have played positive roles in the shaping and reshaping of American economic institutions.

Now we have the news media, and politicians, reinforcing the myth that African American history is Slavery, and not much else. Some in our society consider Americans of African descent as a device of shame, while at the same time they reward them with the Badge of Combat and the Purple Heart. Americans should recoil in horror from the ugliness of this fraudulent compromise provision.

This compromise provision is a legal and religious justification for constitutional apartheid. An official constitutional apology for the Three-Fifths Compromise agreement is truly essential for the economic re-development of this country. We believe that after our virtuous debate on this issue, Americans can, and will, make the right choice.

Who's Living in the Worst Neighborhoods

As citizens, we should detest the cruelty that was created because of the lack of common language, understanding, and consideration of one's ethnicity. The Northern and Western parts of the United States are creating ghettos where ghettos did not exist before. Our ghettos are so violent and crime filled that the L.A.P.D allowed the United State Marines to ride along with them in these ghetto areas. This was done to train the troops on urban combat tactics.

> "But what we can do, as flawed as we are, is still see God in other people, and do our best to help them find their own grace. That's what I strive to do, that's what I pray to do every day
>
> **Barack Obama**

This training demonstrates that both the LAPD, and the United State Marines, believe that our ghettos are good training grounds for learning how to apply war tactics against the Taliban. This compromise has segregated and divided people by color and by their position in life, creating an economic and cultural war zone.

We are hoping that this chapter will enable Americans to grasp the true purpose of the language within the Three-Fifths Compromise agreement. This chapter has allowed you to understand the big picture and how the pieces of our lives fit within the passages of our Constitution. This understanding will not only lessen the strains between us, but will also bridge the economic gap between ethnic groups. Once we appreciate where our wealth stems from, we can make better economic choices.

This nation has the most culturally tolerant young generation in the history of the United States. They are privileged to live in a time of extraordinary medical miracles and communication revolutions that are redefining their lives. Yet we, as a nation, have not managed to end the trauma of the long, drawn-out debate regarding equality.

While most of us are grateful to be living in America, we recognize and agonize that our economic future is being sold to the highest bidder. Despite all of this, our Constitution is closer to perfection for all Americans then we realize. Constitutional perfection is just one amendment away. As a nation, we must take meaningful steps to resolve the issues of poverty, cultural violence, and reverse discrimination.

Fear Within a Nation.

The Three-Fifths Compromise has made this nation, and its citizens, pay horrible economic and social consequences for our Fore-Fathers constitutional transgressions. The unpleasant effect of the Three-Fifths Compromise has plagued our country with cultural violence and economic despair. These unpleasant effects will not stop until we amend this compromise provision. This compromise provision has raped its own citizens of their economic freedoms.

Constitutional insensitivity is the worst form of thoughtlessness. It has allowed this nation to eject various groups of people. The Three-Fifths Compromise has created a growing underclass in American society today. This group of underclass citizens is disproportionately non-Caucasian and disadvantaged Caucasian. They are our native sons and daughters who are filling our courtrooms and jails. They have a different language, separate culture, and separate vision, and they can't envision the real America.

Within the heart and soul of our Constitution's rule of law resides a cultural war of animosity. This cultural war affects each and every American because there are no boundaries beyond its reach. The consequences of this cultural war are found within our homes, our churches, our schools, our work places and within our political system. There are no places to hide from their negative forces.

Presently, we are experiencing this cultural war of ethnic hostility, violence and animosity between citizens. This compromise provision has created a hostile environment within this nation where violence is inescapable. It has been demonstrated throughout this chapter that there will always be a negative cause and effect whenever a nation makes legal choices based on cultural profiling. The cause and the effect of the Three-Fifths Compromise is inexcusable, unreasonable and should be considered a huge lapse in the Founders judgment. That's why, as citizens, we need to protect our Constitution from any and all who would try to abuse its authority.

This will require us to put aside our prejudices and fears and to work together to resolve the issue of the Three-Fifths Compromise agreement. As authors, we believe in our hearts that great things, on an enormous scale, will occur within this nation once this constitutional apology becomes a reality.

We also believe in the sanctity of the Constitution of the United States. We believe that it is the soul and the fabric of the American way of life. It is a living, timeless and compassionate document which brings hope to all who have confidence in its innovative words.

There is scientific evidence that leads one to accept as true, that everything in our universe was created for a specific reason. And within that reasoning our thoughts and dreams were set in motion. Everything that we morally believe in, and can imagine, has an invisible source which we, as mortal men, cannot alter nor fully appreciate. This invisible source is the realization of God by man.

Everything that man can see, touch, and change comes from a different source. It too was created for a specific reason. This source is the realization of man governing man. Man can alter and utilize this source for his own existence. The Constitution of the United States is that source. It alone is what guarantees our freedom and gives us a sense of hope and honor.

The Constitutional rule of law, which we all enjoy and are governed by, is not as perfect as the realization of God. However, at the core of the Constitution's foundation are the theories of True Conservatism. It is what brings out the best in America.

REVERSE DISCRIMINATION
THE BOOMERANG EFFECT

This chapter, "Reverse Discrimination: The Boomerang Effect", will reveal the source of reverse discrimination, as well as its economic, physical, sociological and psychological impacts on our society. Both political parties utilize allegations of reverse discrimination as a blunt instrument to protect the status-quo. These politicians are now in the midst of capturing the mind and soul of Americans. They misuse and misapply the phrase; 'reverse discrimination' for their own political gain.

> "America will never be destroyed from the outside. If we falter and lose our freedoms, it will be because we destroyed ourselves.."
>
> **Abraham Lincoln**

What is reverse discrimination and how is it initiated? Who is being hurt by it, and what can be done to reverse its negative economic impact on America? As we answer these questions, allow us to reveal how reverse discrimination actually started.

Historically, cultural discrimination, or reverse discrimination, was primarily directed toward people based on the color of their skin. Reverse discrimination is not a new phenomenon in America. This phenomenon is the side-effect of cultural discrimination, functioning in reverse. Cultural discrimination is the side-effect of the apartheid languages within the Three-Fifths Compromise agreement.

Reverse Discrimination Does Exist

The foundational language of the Three-Fifths Compromise was based on the theory of cultural profiling, thereby reversing the victim's constitutional privileges. We will demonstrate throughout this chapter that the compromise provision is the source which introduced cultural profiling within the Constitution. The phenomenon reverse discrimination, does exist, and is the chief cause of economic disparity among ethnic groups.

Both cultural and reverse discrimination are the unconstitutional side-effects of this compromise provision. What some Caucasian men are feeling today in the workplace with regard to discrimination is legitimate. Though the correct legal phrase for what they are presently experiencing is not reverse discrimination, but cultural discrimination functioning in reverse. Presently, because of the boomerang effects of the Three-Fifths Compromise, Caucasian men have now joined the ranks of other ethnic groups, who have felt the devastating side effect of this compromise for hundreds of years.

> "As I would not be a slave, so I would not be a master. This expresses my idea of democracy."
>
> **Abraham Lincoln**

However, because of the boomerang effect of the compromise provision on middle class Caucasian males, the United States Supreme Court and Congress are allowing new cultural profiling laws to be enacted. These new rulings by the Supreme Court are an attempt to fix, what they know to be, the disturbing facts about this compromise. This form of constitutional discrimination can only be corrected through repealing/amending the Three-Fifths compromise provision.

The Origin of Cultural Discrimination.

Throughout this book, the term Three-Fifths Compromise provision has been exposed as the enemy of the people. This compromise provision is the origin of cultural and reverse discrimination. It is anti-American and is a disease on our social infrastructure. The purpose for this 1787 compromise provision was to deprive constitutional rights and economic privileges to a certain ethnic group. This compromise was initiated to manipulate the victim's free-will, as well as to suppress their voices and their votes. It also separates them from any chance of creating intergenerational transfer of wealth for their descendents.

This compromise provision was, and still is, unconstitutional! Cultural and reverse discrimination are two of the harmful side effects of the Three-Fifths Compromise. This compromise is now affecting millions of Americans' civil liberties, regardless of their ethnicity, age or sex.

The primary and legal purpose behind the Three-Fifths Compromise agreement was to keep the word "slavery" from appearing within the language of the Constitution. The act of slavery, in and of itself, is not the focus of this book. The only reason the word "slavery" is brought up is because the language of the Three-Fifths Compromise itself is a form of constitutional enslavement. The design of this compromise permitted our government to evade legal, psychological and economic responsibility for the continuance of slavery until 1865.

The thirteenth amendment to the U.S. Constitution is what finally abolished the physical side of slavery. Although, the psychological and the economic side effects of slavery still live within the official language of this compromise contract with America. The language of this compromise is a constitutional contract between the Northern and Southern states. This contract stated that the total number of dark ethnic groups from Africa was constitutionally deemed to be three-fifths of its total population.

Thereby, three-fifths of this population was not constitutionally equal to the whole of the privileged European population. This reversal of Due Process, and versal of Due Process, and the Civil Liberties for these groups, has led to the economic and social predicament that we, as a nation, face.

> *I desire so to conduct the affairs of this administration that if at the end... I have lost every other friend on earth, I shall at least have one friend left, and that friend shall be down inside of me."*
>
> **Abraham Lincoln**

The founders recognized that the word "slavery" could not appear within the Constitution. It was known that this word; "slavery", would have been a reversal of the basic premise to the fundamental theory of True Conservatism. Consciously, they wanted to establish a document that would be flexible in the event that slavery was ever abolished.

The Three-Fifths Compromise agreement provided the Founders with an extraordinary way to avoid the occurrence of any constitutional crisis after slavery was ended. Presently, this nation is in the midst of both a constitutional and an economic crisis, just as the Founders had feared. This compromise provision is having an adverse effect on every segment of our population. It is causing each ethnic group to feel the 'boomerang' effects of cultural and reverse discrimination in the workplace and in our schools.

Is This Compromise Provision a Law?

The Three-Fifths Compromise was inserted into Article I Section 2 Paragraph 3 of the United States Constitution as a by-law/ *agreement.* It is actually a constitutional agreement based on cultural profiling. This compromise is a betrayal to the theory of True Conservatism. It is this compromise provision that threatens our national economic stability. It has allowed for inequality to materialize within the rule of law and in the workplace.

This compromise is in complete opposition to the spirit of our liberty and must be repealed. It must not be left unresolved or set aside. If this compromise is left unrepaired, it alone will continue to reverse all of our civil liberties and our economic-wellness to the point of no return. It has created a two hundred year gap of lost economic prosperity for the population for who it was fashioned.

The total essence of the Three-Fifths Compromise is the raping of one's individual civil liberties and their economic wealth. It is the illegal and immoral part of our Constitution. This compromise provision was installed for the express purpose of legally seizing control of a certain ethnic group's self-worth and future wealth.

At this moment in time, the after affects of this compromise provision are raping America of her self-worth. It is an open wound and a cancer on the soul of this nation. This compromise provision is eating away at the fabric of this nation's foundation and is affecting not only the individual person, but the nation's conscience as well. It has made it nearly impossible for the victims of this compromise provision to ever catch up economically.

The Three-Fifths Compromise is a form of constitutional rape. It is a psychological, emotional and a legal form of rape in which the victims are forced to surrender their birth rights and their family names. As previously mentioned, this compromise has exposed the victims to political scams, with their futures being sold to the highest bidder.

Whatever you call this compromise provision, whether it is cultural discrimination or reverse discrimination, it really doesn't matter. It is still a form of constitutional rape. Presently, this compromise provision is causing all Americans to feel the unpleasant rippling effects of its unconstructive power.

The Three-Fifths Compromise agreement is constitutional discrimination in and of itself. It is the taking away of one's civil liberties, without regard to the color of one's skin, political opinion or sexual orientation. Simply put, constitutional discrimination is our Constitution working in reverse, for certain segments of the population.

This compromise provision allowed for the bending and reshaping of our constitutional rule of law. It made a part of our Constitution unacceptable, which helped establish a wave of favoritism giving rise to the "Boomerang Effects" of reverse discrimination.

The only clear first step to eliminating cultural and reverse discrimination, within the Constitution, is to begin the debates on how to amend this passage. This debate should have occurred years ago when Congress first became aware of its effects on the people. Congress decided it to be a moot/ *unresolved* position. It had no practical economic value for them.

> *If the people cannot trust their government to do the job for which it exists to protect them and to promote their common welfare - all else is lost.*
>
> **Barack Obama**

Presently, neither political party wants to discuss this nation's legal obligation to pay restitution for its inhumane treatment to a certain segment of this nation's population. It would be economically unprofitable for Congress to actually debate the real source of cultural and reverse discrimination in this country. Nevertheless, because of the boomerang effects of cultural discrimination, there are many Americans of European descent who are experiencing firsthand the economic and emotional pains of cultural discrimination in their lives.

Experiencing Reverse Discrimination

I, too, have been a victim of cultural and reverse discrimination throughout the course my life. Although, the reverse discrimination that my siblings and I have to endure is on a grander scale. Knowing where the pain of reverse discrimination is coming from does not make it any easier for the victims to deal with. Reverse discrimination is not a cultural illusion, it does exist and here are some legitimate examples.

However, before we continue, I would like to formally introduce myself, and give you a firsthand account of my own experiences with cultural and reverse discrimination. I can, in all fairness, share these experiences with you because my life, in its entirety, has revolved around its negative effects. My name is Robert Gates, author of this book. I first felt the anxiety of cultural and reverse discrimination, at the tender age of eleven, with my family's decision to move to an all Caucasian suburb in Gary, Indiana.

When we began our move it was late at night. I didn't understand why we moved so late, though I would soon find out the next day. I woke up around six the following morning. I got up from the bed and ran to the window to see my new surroundings. First, I saw three beautiful green baseball fields in a row. Second, I saw something that I had never seen before in my life. There were no persons of color at all, just white people everywhere. In those few moments my life as I had known it, was forever changed.

Two days later, I asked my older brother, "Where are we"? He said that we now lived in an all white community, and that things would be better for us as a family. My mom told me that we will receive a better education here. At the age of eleven, what did I care about getting a better education, there was nothing wrong with me. My parents enrolled me in Wirt High School in 1967, where I started the seventh grade. It didn't take long for me to realize that of the thirteen hundred enrolled students, I was one of ten students of color.

My first experience with cultural and reverse discrimination happened that very first day of school. Walking to school on that first day I got awfully thirsty and headed for the nearest water fountain. I took my place in line and waited my turn. As I was about to take a sip of water, I was pulled by the ear by a school staff member. I was told I was standing in the wrong line. He said that I had to go to the water fountain designated for colored people. I couldn't do or say anything; I was at a loss for words. What was wrong with the color of my skin? Why couldn't I drink out of the same fountain as everyone else? I couldn't understand this separation by color. It was all new and frightening to me. All I knew was that before I moved to this new place I didn't have any problems drinking from the same water fountain as the other kids.

That morning, for the first time in my life, I was stunned into the realization that for some reason, the color of my skin was going to be an obstacle for me. This was the first of many cultural and reverse discrimination experiences that have had an adverse effect on my assessment of life.

This new awareness was painful, offensive, and made my life tremendously unpredictable. The illusion of color forever changed my outlook on life. My childlike expectations turned from excitement and enthusiasm into pains of despair.

The Pain of Cultural Rejection

This rejection, because of my skin color, became more obvious as I was placed in the most dilapidated chair in the back of each classroom. Most of my seventh grade teachers didn't answer my questions or acknowledge me when I raised my hand in class. As the days turned into months, I began to ask myself what was happening to my life and my education.

My mom had said that we moved here because they had excellent schools. If that were true, why was I so far behind in my education? I didn't have any answers. When my teachers did call on me in class, they asked me to empty the trash, erase the chalk board, run errands to the principal's office, or to sharpen someone else's pencil.

Throughout the course of that year, I was beaten-up at least once every two weeks for making acquaintances with white girls or for being at the wrong place at the wrong time. I had to fight as I walked to and from school, class to class and during lunch almost every other day. My attacker's only reason for attacking me was because of the color of my skin. All of this running and hiding placed unjustifiable stress on me, taking its toll on my body and my psyche.

It seems to me that there shouldn't have been any reason for a thirteen year old boy to have to go through this kind of discrimination. I quickly learned in the ninth grade that I must become skilled at assimilating into main stream society, just as I had seen white women do at school.

I made it my mission in life to walk, talk, dress and dance like white kids. I made as many Caucasian friends as I possibly could, for my own protection. For a while this worked. My assimilation efforts seemed to be paying off. In the middle of the tenth grade I was allowed to go to dances and football games without the fear of being assaulted, and it even seemed that my grades were improving.

Then to my surprise, by the eleventh grade I was allowed to join the school's wresting team. It felt good to be the first young man of color on the team. I knew from past experience that I would have to work harder than my peers to keep my varsity position. That was no problem for me, because I knew that I was learning how to play the hand that was dealt to me in this country.

One particular evening we had a wrestling match at an all white high school. Prior to each match it was customary for the wrestlers to shake hands. That night my dreams of equality and my hard work of assimilating began to fade away. It all began when my opponent refused to shake my hand. I returned to the bench and the people in the stands pointed at me with disgust. I felt degraded. I had experienced the pains of rejection many times before, but not to such an extreme.

As I looked to my coach for sympathy and answers, he looked around the gymnasium, then at the referees and after a few seconds he turns to me. He looked me in the eye and ,with dismay, said to me, "I'm sorry Robert, but your opponent does not want to have body contact with you because you're black". I was so saddened by his response that I wanted to yell, "What is wrong with me?"

At this point in my life, I was well acquainted with many forms of rejection and the pain and disappointment that came with it. But this time it was different. I had worked hard to get on and to stay on the team. I had struggled to assimilate into their world of privileges. In the end, my efforts to assimilate were halted all because of a non-handshake.

I felt that my coach had not stood up to the referees and made it clear that it was only fair that if I didn't wrestle in this match because of my color, no one else on the squad would be able to participate. Instead, I was told to go to the locker room, remove my wrestling uniform and to hand it over to my Caucasian team mate, who would wrestle in my place.

I looked at the coach with surprise and asked "why"? My team mate hadn't earned my position; yet he got to wrestle in my place because his skin is white and I get booed because mine is not. What happened to me that evening is something that I cannot even describe. It wasn't racism; to me it was just down to earth spitefulness, in the oldest sense. This type of rejection was so painful that I cried off and on for about two weeks.

Rules for Success in Reverse

I knew from that moment on, it didn't matter how hard I tried to assimilate, I would have to use a different approach to get the things I needed and wanted in this country. The constitutional rules for success in this country were reversed for me. The good thing about this realization was, at least I knew the rules.

This meant that for my future, I would have to take firm action to make things happen. I became a firm believer that you can make things happen, or let things happen. The one thing that I loved most about being in this school was the reciting of the Pledge of Allegiance. Each morning that I would say this pledge gave me inspiration to learn the laws that governed my life

I graduated from Wirt high school at the age of nineteen. Out of a class of 275 students, I was proud to be number 85 in rank. I was fully aware that the laws of success were stacked against me. This country still bore the scars and the remnants of slavery past's and I carried the remnants of a slave's name. My color excluded me from becoming a member of the good old boys network.

The question for me was how do I become successful in my life with all of these constitutional barriers? I discovered that my civil liberties were working in reverse for me. Knowing this fact affected my outlook on life. It affected me to the point that, at times, when I looked in the mirror, I often wondered how my life would have been different had I been born white, with all the constitutional privileges afforded to me.

> "A rooster crows only when it sees the light. Put him in the dark and he'll never crow. I have seen the light and I'm crowing."
>
> **Muhammad Ali**

My early life's experiences with cultural and reverse discrimination taught me that there are always two sides to every dilemma in this nation. That it is up to me, not my government or the people around me, to find out which solution would work the best for me. I discovered that the solutions to my problems were in the noble parts of the Constitution, where the color of my skin and my economic status would not have any bearing on my civil liberties. I was hopeful that this noble document would put an end to the boomerang effects of discrimination in my life, and that of others.

The Effects of Cultural Discrimination

At nineteen, I knew where I stood in this country. I knew, in order for me to achieve any business goals, my plans for success needed to be plotted out differently than that of the status quo. I needed to find a way to get beyond the effects of reverse and cultural discrimination.

Through those struggling years, I have learned that the only thing standing between me and my success was not just slavery's past or the Three-Fifths Compromise agreement. It was also my perspective on life. My expectations for success had to be high, and I knew that by the grace of God, I could not fail. I could achieve anything in my life regardless of the laws which were intended to hold me back.

However, because of my life experiences dealing with reverse discrimination and rejection, I've found that there is always a silver lining to any madness! I've discovered how to deal with rejection in a proactive way. I have found that by reversing the mental pain

A popular government without popular information or the means of acquiring it, is but a prologue to a farce, or a tragedy, or perhaps both.

James Madison

of rejection and turning it back on to the victimizer, has allowed me to free myself from their games of spitefulness. It also gave me the upper hand in any offensive situation that came my way. This approach to rejection gave me total control over my life. These discriminatory experiences made me learn early in life to never be the victim, or play the victim, in any situation.

As said earlier, reverse discrimination and cultural discrimination was initiated with the addition of the Three-Fifths Compromise to the Constitution. This compromise was formed to insure that certain Caucasian

> *"If once you forfeit the confidence of your fellow-citizens, you can never regain their respect and esteem."*
>
> **Abraham Lincoln**

men, from the Northern or Southern states, held the best jobs in this nation. It alone, reversed the true fundamentals of our liberties.

For any American to continue their denial of the existent of cultural or reverse discrimination is hateful and offensive. This compromise provision was purposely hidden in Article One. It was designed to deceive Americans of its true agenda. The real problem Americans of European descent face, in the workforce today, is not reverse discrimination. What they are actually facing is the boomerang effect of the insertion of this compromise provision into the Constitution.

The Controversy over Affirmative Action

Our Constitution, along with affirmative action programs, are only effective if all Americans, regardless of their ethnicity, can benefit from them. The Three-Fifths Compromise provision has constitutionally provided Caucasian males, in this country, a two hundred year economic advantage over non-Caucasians and women.

This compromise provision is solely based on cultural profiling. This allowed the European Caucasian males to dominate the constitutional rule of law, which gave them unfettered constitutional privileges. The foundational language designed for the Three-Fifths Compromise agreement was calculated at best! The Founders deliberately based part of their constitutional authority on the whiteness of someone's skin and their cultural common belief.

The opposition to affirmative action, and those who believe they are being discriminated against, is basing their entire legal argument on the color of their skin. They are conveniently forgetting that the legal criteria for affirmative action is race, disability, gender, ethnic origin, and age. There are no policies within affirmative action that are purposely designed to punish Americans of European descent, because of their skin color.

Though the total opposite is true of the Three-Fifths Compromise provision. Its sole purpose is to deny constitutional liberties to a certain segment of the population, based on one's color. Affirmative action policies have been instituted in schools, universities and corporations. This action was taken by President John F. Kennedy in order to bring about cultural constitutional balance within these institutions. President John F. Kennedy had the constitutional foresight to take legal steps to correct past injustices, by employing affirmative action in 1961.

There are those politicians who are opposed to affirmative action policies, for political and cultural reasons. They claim that these policies provide unfair consideration to the Caucasian population. Opponents of affirmative action also believe that affirmative action programs have gone too far, and have become nothing more than discrimination in reverse. Yet, affirmative action was designed to protect all ethnic groups, including Americans of European descent. The controversy over affirmative action policies, and reverse discrimination, are often at the center of heated immigration debates.

Supporters of affirmative action point out that these policies set diversified goals, rather than quotas. Affirmative Action will level the playing fields to give the historically disadvantaged a chance to catch up. The supporters of affirmative action also claim that reverse discrimination is nothing more than a myth. As authors, we have proven that this statements is far from the truth.

Opponents of affirmative action continue to argue that there aren't any logical differences between "goals" and "quotas". It is argued that affirmative action programs do not promote diversity for employment, but do encourage bias based on color. Some claim that non-Caucasian Americans should be judged on their individual merits, without the injection of cultural considerations.

We agree with the assessment of the opponents of affirmative action, that applicants should be judged by their individual merits. We also want to be clear on the meaning of the term *"goal"*. In accordance with Webster's dictionary, the word "goal" is the opposite of the word "quota". The purposes of a goal, in affirmative action policies, were to establish achievable reference points of fair play within our society. The writers of affirmative action programs view the setting of quotas as an unconstitutional act. It was their purpose to establish fair play in the workplace. Individuals who are opposed to these policies continue to talk about quotas by engaging in their own falsehoods.

> *"Government exists to protect us from each other. Where government has gone beyond its limits is in deciding to protect us from ourselves."*
>
> **Ronald Reagan**

The opposition to affirmative action want to establish that an overwhelming number of minorities have already achieved a high level of equality in the workplace. It seems; opponents of affirmative action are the only ones who want to set quotas on how many victims can, or should, be helped for past cultural and economic discrimination. How can anyone in our society put a true estimate on how long it will take to correct a two hundred year economic gap between ethnic groups?

The sincere question in these debates should be; how many years will it take to even the playing fields? The Three-Fifths Compromise passage has been in existence for over two hundred years. Fifty years of affirmative action programs cannot possibly undo the economic damages that has occurred.

It may take another sixty years or more to level the playing field in the workplace. That is the reason the writers of affirmative action set goals for their policies rather than quotas. If opponents of affirmative action cannot understand the concept between goals and quotas, it is simply because they do not want to. It doesn't take a rocket scientist to figure this out.

How Is Reverse Discrimination Affecting You?

It has been acknowledged, and proven, that certain Caucasian citizens are now experiencing the boomerang effects of past cultural discriminatory actions. Yet, while cultural discrimination in the workplace is new to this group, more will feel its effects in the coming years. As we previously stated, the real problem that Caucasian men are facing in the workplace is not reverse discrimination. The proper legal phrase for what they are experiencing is cultural discrimination, functioning in reverse.

The opponents of affirmative action cannot productively discuss reverse discrimination cases with just the reference to color. Making legal statements such as; "I am a victim of reverse discrimination because I am a white male", is a false and misleading legal argument. That seems to be the main, if not the only, argument of their law suits. Not once have the opponents of affirmative action shown any legal document stating their claims of exclusion. And, why haven't Caucasian women filed lawsuits stating that they are also experiencing reverse discrimination?

It must be acknowledged that affirmative action programs are not the source, or the vehicle, that drives the effects of reverse discrimination. The source of reverse discrimination, and the vehicle that is the driving force behind it, is the Three-Fifths Compromise provision. Affirmative action programs have been written as compensatory acts for past injustices, and not for the protection of people based on their color. Reverse discrimination has been called by the opponents of affirmative action "reverse racism" or "activist discrimination".

The term "reverse discrimination" should not be considered as a racist term, for it's a legal term that originated, and was developed, through the language within the Constitution. It does imply that one must belong to a historically disadvantaged group to be culturally discriminated against.

The problem with this assumption is that Americans of European descent have not yet been exposed to the full constraints of cultural discrimination in the workplace. The debates on affirmative action must include the repeal of the Three-Fifths Compromise concession. If not, there is no genuine debate.

Opponents of affirmative action may continue to criticize and question the fairness of this legislation. However, they must come to the realization that the language they use in describing affirmative action policies are quite offensive. It is also insincere and inappropriate for politicians

> *To suppose that any form of government will secure liberty or happiness without any virtue in the people, is a chimerical idea.*
>
> **James Madison**

and their lawyers to continue using color as their only legal argument against affirmative action programs.

Is Reverse Discrimination a Myth?

Without any doubt, reverse-discrimination is not a myth. It does exist in many forms, and is now affecting all men and women in the workplace, regardless of their ethnicity.

The opponents of affirmative action claim that affirmative action programs are not necessary any more, but they are dead wrong. Today, American Caucasians are the latest ethnic group who now need to utilize the protection of affirmative action because of the boomerang effects of the Three-Fifths Compromise.

Some politicians, who are opponents of affirmative action, have stated, "If we were a color blind society, there would not be any discrimination on the basis of color, sex or age in this country". Though after two hundred years of the elite dominating the nation's rule of law by color, they now desire a color blind society! They think that a color blind society is the solution to preventing cultural and reverse discrimination from affecting their descendents.

Thank God most of us live in reality. Our Constitution's rule of law was not designed to practice, or uphold, the rule of law under a color-blind society. The foundational language of Three-Fifths Compromise was built on the basis of one's undesirable skin color.

Therefore, the theory of a color-blind society sounds good, but it bears no weight in these debates. Not until the Three-Fifths Compromise issue is dealt with, can we honestly debate on how to prevent cultural and reverse discrimination from occurring.

Opponents of affirmative action always disagree on how to bring up, or debate, past cultural and reverse discrimination injustices. The status-quo, and their descendents, have never been the victims of constitutional discrimination in the workplace on a massive scale in this country.

Therefore, this talk of a color blind society is an illusion. It is another way the politicians interject taboo words, such as; 'racism' or 'playing the race card'. These phrases seem to be some politician's favorite words when attacking their opponents.

The non-Caucasian population, and women, have been mistreated in the past for a morally irrelevant characteristic. This irrelevant characteristic was that they had a darker skin color, or they were the weaker sex. To say that affirmative action programs were written to give preferential treatment for the same morally irrelevant characteristic is equally indefensible, it is actually an insult.

There seems to be a miscalculation by the politicians between what is said to be their supremacy of cultural common knowledge beliefs and what has happened historically. The idea that preferential treatment should not be given to people because of their color is one thing. To say people of color should not be given fair treatment in the workplace; because of previous mistreatment by our government, is another.

Our nation has a long tradition of awarding compensatory damages to its victims because of governmental mistreatment. Why should our policies of awarding compensatory damages change now? Americans of African descent and disadvantaged Caucasians in this country, including aliens, both resident and illegal, are at an economic disadvantage because of this flawed compromise provision.

The opponents of affirmative action, and the status quo, are determined to project the illusion of race into our society. The language of the Three-Fifths Compromise theorizes that the African population was an unsuitable feature and that these victims of this inhumane agreement were only worth three-fifths of their total.

The boomerang effect of this compromise has placed the majority of Americans into some form of economic bondage. Yet no politician today has the foresight or the confidence to speak-up and take action against this fraudulent language.

Affirmative action has never justified preferential treatment on the basis of one's race or color. It is justifiable on the basis of past mistreatment of a people because of their ethnicity or gender. Supporters of affirmative action do not believe that being a non-Caucasian is a morally relevant feature that deserves compensation for discriminatory conduct. They do believe that injustices based on that conduct should be compensated. To compensate a group of people because of their skin color is unconstitutionally. Although to compensate an ethnic group for past cultural injustices is constitutionally justifiable.

Color Blind Society?

Opponents of affirmative action claim that the best society is a color-blind society. If this is true, they should be the first to debate the lack of compensation based on past constitutional wrongs. Instead, the opponents of affirmative action are debating whether affirmative action programs are the right method for correcting past and present injustices.

This compromise provision presently insures that a color-blind society is not possible. In our view, an official apology for the Three-Fifths Compromise would be an act of courage that will determine the heart and soul of our nation.

The status quo continues to debate reverse discrimination from a color blind perspective, but has failed to include solutions for cultural discrimination itself. Opponents of affirmative action expect you to believe that there are no differences between the victims of past cultural and reverse discrimination and the victims of today.

Even Congress continues to pass laws on the basis of color and gender, which have universal support and approval from both sides of the aisle. Among these laws are the 13th Amendment, which abolished slavery, and the 15th and 19th amendments, which gave Americans of African descent and women the right to vote. All three amendments are based on the reversal of cultural profiling.

> *The truth is that all men having power ought to be mistrusted.*
>
> **James Madison**

The essence of this compromise provision, along with reverse discrimination, stem from the very same source, our Constitution. These issues can only be settled through sound debates and not by crafty rhetoric. The Federal Courts enforcement of affirmative action programs, which were well overdue, terminated the advantages of the status quo and their descendants. These enforcements of Due Process for all citizens are not an abuse of constitutional power. It is justice for a non-color blind society, which the opponents of affirmative action's ancestors helped to facilitate.

Wealth at the Expense of Others

Many people of upper and middle economic positions are sensitive to the dilemmas of those of lower economic status. It is those within the status quo who shut down emotionally, when they hear the words affirmative action or entitlements.

Though the Civil Rights Act was enacted in 1964, it fell short of economically helping the victims of the Three-Fifths Compromise agreement. The opponents of affirmative action and Congress refused to admit to the historical acts of cultural preferences. They continue to pretend that past constitutional discrimination is not their responsibility to correct.

Here are some examples of the status quo's own version of earlier types of affirmative action programs, that worked in their favor. In 1790, Congress enacted the Naturalization Act. This biased program allowed for free European immigrants to become naturalized citizens, but it excluded those who were not Caucasians. The Naturalization Act was replaced by the Mc-Carran-Walter Act in 1952. By this time, the economic damage caused by this act was already widespread.

With a large number of free European immigrants coming to this nation there was a need for more land. This encouraged the enactment of the Indian Removal Act of 1830. The Cherokee, the Creek, and other Native Americans, who were the original settlers of this country, were forcibly driven off their ancestral lands.

With the help of the U.S. Military, the Native Americans were pushed west of the Mississippi River to unproductive barren lands to make room for European Immigrants. Ultimately, 270 million acres of Indian Territory west of the Mississippi, or 10% of the total land area of the United States, was transferred into the hands of the status quo.

Then there was the Homestead Act, which was signed by President Abraham Lincoln on May 20, 1862. The Homestead Act encouraged Western migration by providing only European settlers 160 acres of public land. In exchange, homesteaders paid a small filing fee and were required to complete five years of continuous residence before receiving ownership of the land. Homesteaders also had the option of purchasing the land from the government at $1.25 per acre after six months of residency. This Homestead Act led to the distribution of 80 million acres of public land by 1900.

Let's not forget the states Jim Crow laws, which were based on cultural profiling. These barbaric laws were instituted in the late 19th and the early 20th centuries. These laws were enacted to reserve the best of jobs, neighborhoods, schools and hospitals for the status quo. These laws were not federally overturned until the early 1960's, in many states. These states Jim Crow laws have provided economic, and constitutional, advantages to Caucasian Americans from generation to generation.

The most recent and least known of these congressional entitlements, which were designed purposely for Caucasian

Americans, were enacted with the New Deal programs of the 1930's. These programs were designed to direct wealth and opportunities to those who color was considered white.

There also was the landmark Social Security Act of 1935, which provided a safety net for millions in the workforce. This Act guaranteed Americans of European descent an income after retirement. Agricultural workers and domestic servants were two occupations specifically excluded, since this work employed predominately African Americans, Latinos, Asians, or women. These low-income workers did not have the opportunity to save for their retirement, nor could they leave any inheritance to their children.

The Wagner Act, like the Social Security Act, helped to establish the collective bargaining power of the worker's unions. These unions helped millions of Americans of European descent to become middle class families for their fore seen future. The acquirement of these rewards, because of cultural preferences, was wrong then and, by all accounts, is constitutionally wrong now.

The consequences of preferential treatment for the descendents of the status quo have economically devastated non-Caucasians. The average Caucasian American today, through no fault of their own, has eight times the resources, or net worth, than the typical non- Caucasian family. This is according to economist Edward Wolff. These examples of past cultural preferences show the existence of hypocrisy on the part of current congressional leaders. Opponents of affirmative action are claiming that Caucasian males are being discriminated against in the workplace. They have collectively based their entire legal argument on the premise that, because of their skin color, they are being discriminated against.

But not once have the opponents of affirmative action shown any legal documentation that proves their case. This legal charge against affirmative action is fraudulent, at best.

These lawmakers are purposely overlooking the real enemy to Caucasian males in the workplace. As we have proven throughout this book, the enemy in question is the Three-Fifths Compromise agreement.

Intergenerational Transfer of Wealth

A family's net worth is not simply the bottom line; it is also the starting point of the intergenerational transfer of wealth to their following generations. Those families, who have wealth, pass their assets on to their children through the financing of a college education, lending their children a hand during hard times, or assisting them with a down payment towards buying a new home.

Some economists have estimated that up to 80 percent of one's lifetime of accumulated wealth is dependent upon these intergenerational transfers of wealth. The families with wealth are able to pass the advantages of wealth from generation to generation. Families who are economically at a disadvantage cannot pass down any wealth to the next generation, although they do pass down their cycle of economic brokenness.

Controlling Wealth by Skin Color

Our government and social institutions were created with the powerful ideas of governing with one's cultural beliefs, and by color. These ideas gave the architects of these laws access to opportunities that would disproportionately channel wealth, power, and resources to their own ethnic group. This chapter has identified these institutional practices and social policies that give advantages to some people, at the expense of others.

The opponents of affirmative action like to pretend that a color blind society would establish equality. A color blind society, if even possible, would not end bigotry or intolerance, nor would it end reverse or cultural discrimination. For no one is born prejudiced; therefore bigotry and intolerance are learned behaviors and not biological

Affirmative action policies were designed to help level the playing field for all Americans, regardless of their ethnicity. But one must admit that affirmative action programs could be re-shaped and reformed to work more efficiently for the 21st century workforce.

In conclusion, there are no actual blueprints that would minimize the negative effects of cultural profiling. Neither are there any blue-prints that would halt the negative effects of the Three-Fifths Compromise within the Constitution. However, as a nation, we are learning

> *"The probability that we may fail in the struggle ought not to deter us from the support of a cause we believe to be just."*
>
> **Abraham Lincoln**

how to resolve some of our cultural and economic problems by using, as a guide, the noble parts of the Constitution.

Every citizen within this nation is being affected, in some way, by the negative influence of the Three-Fifths Com-promise. Where there is a negative reaction, there is al-ways a positive solution. Therefore, we must continue to press forward in this country on the issues of fairness in the workplace.

Our faith should not be in the actions of men, nor in their programs, but in the noble parts of our Constitution. The real question for all Americans should be: what is really needed to level the playing fields in the workplace? The answer is; repeal-ing the Three-Fifths Compromise agreement.

Citizens have been awarded the rights, and the privileges, to live vicariously through the timeless and living words of our Constitution. It is our job and our responsibility, as citizens, to overcome these discriminatory challenges and achieve the perfection within this living document. We must appreciate our Constitution's authority. For the hopes, dreams, and prosperity of all Americans lie within its intent.

DECEPTION OF ENTITLEMENT

"Deception of Entitlement" begins with the examination of the incoherent nature of our country's immigration and naturalization policies. These assessments are based on facts and not on political rhetoric.

This chapter will show how our immigration laws are constitutionally flawed,

> "America is the only country that went from barbarism to decadence without civilization in between."
>
> **Oscar Wilde**

illogical and perplexing, thereby denying and reversing citizenship to millions of people. We will also focus on the unfairness and the lack of equality that have been established within our taxation policies.

The fundamental natures of our immigration, naturalization and taxation policies are structured around the fraudulent languages of the Three-Fifths Compromise agreement. This compromise provision is the ultimate in policymaker's vanity. It was the Founding Fathers exploiting their cultural supremacy. The era of cultural dominance and the illusion of race are over. No more will this nation govern men by one's cultural belief.

Presently, our immigration policies are based on the theories of cultural profiling. These policies were designed to reverse the petitioner's legal right to become a citizen. Because of the Three-Fifths Compromise agreement, the foundation of our naturalization policies must be re-examined.

Who are The Real Americans

America has become a multi-ethnic society. Therefore, why should a person's ethnicity and cultural beliefs be the criteria for the policies of immigration and naturalization? And, what is the effect of the Three-Fifths Compromise on the foundation of our immigration policies? The bottom line is; those of us

> *"The assertion that all men are created equal" was of no practical use in effecting our separation from Great Britain and it was placed in the Declaration not for that, but for future use."*
>
> **Abraham Lincoln**

who are not Native Americans or descendents of slaves are the descendants of immigrants who freely immigrated to this country. The sole question for all Americans should be; when will we finally have serious dialogue on changing our immigration, naturalization and taxation policies?

These dialogues must include realistic solutions to the growing disparity of citizenship between ethnic groups entering this nation. We must have a proactive approach, with the intent of turning these immigration policies from a war on the illegal alien, to a pro-immigration and naturalization course of action. Presently, our immigration and naturalization laws are unconstitutional since they are based on the color of a person's skin, as well as that person's cultural beliefs. New immigration laws are necessary for the twenty-first century America.

The common goal of immigration policies in this nation should be of benefit to the government and its citizens. It should also give hope to anyone who desires to come to our shores. The cultural common knowledge approaches, to our nation's immigration laws, are inconsistent and unsuitable for a multi- ethnic society.

These flawed immigration policies have negatively influenced our legal system. There is a double standard within our nation's immigration and naturalization policies brought on by a cultural mind set. These policies have not allowed for the process of assimilation and intergenerational transfer of wealth for millions of Americans.

Is The Term 'Minority' Offensive?

This nation is a nation of immigrants, a pool of people classified by the status quo as minorities, who have now become the majority. And, as a nation, we must become aware of the fact that Americans of European descent have now joined the ranks of the majority of minorities. The fact of the matter is, the term "minority" is an offensive term. It should not be utilized within our courts or our educational systems. It is an illusionary term designed by past legislators who deemed a particular group of people within society as socially, physically and mentally inferior. The status quo also used the term *minorities* when they legally declared Americans of African descent as less than three-fifth of a person.

It is time that our nation's immigration and naturalization laws reflect the needs of all its citizens and not just those of the status quo. It is our belief that without a realistic solution to our nation's policies on immigration and naturalization, violence and animosity will escalate and become more brutal between ethnic groups.

This nation's flawed naturalization process should not be the determining factor to one's financial status or one's role as a citizen. Today's immigration and naturalization policies are a major constitutional hurdle for millions. It is imperative that we do not take these flawed immigration policies for granted. The income of every American household is affected by these defective policies. Our country's growing diversity requires a plan for sharing in the responsibilities of wealth and power. To accomplish this goal, we must determine if our immigration policies are governed by the noble language of our Constitution or by the status quo.

What is The Politically Correct Color?

There are many government bureaucrats, at both federal and state levels, who are carrying out our immigration and naturalization policies with a dogmatic mentality. They have made it clear to the world that if you are not born white, which is said to be the politically correct skin color, you have little or no value in America.

> *"As I would not be a slave, so I would not be a master. This expresses my idea of democracy."*
>
> **Abraham Lincoln**

There are many Republicans, and some Democrats, that do not consider Barack Obama, our forty-fourth President of the United States, to be an American born citizen. They would like to use the immigration and naturalization policies to remove him from office. President Obama is biracial, but is labeled by the Census Bureau as only being black, denying the existence of his Caucasian heritage.

The immigration and naturalization agency has; for over 100 years, utilized the Three-Fifths Compromise agreement, along with the Black Code laws, to constitutionally deny millions of citizens their civil liberties. The Black Code policies of the United

States stated that if a person is one-quarter of African descent, they are to be constitutionally labeled as a Negro, or felons. The Black Codes were laws that were passed by most State governments during the Democratic Presidency of Andrew Johnson.

These new state laws, the Black Codes, were the new methods of legal servitude. This was also the Southern States way of rejecting and challenging the constitutionality of the 13th and 14th amendments. This new form of institutionalized slavery was brought about by the fears of men in search for cultural dominance.

Freedom to Assimilate and Integrate

The Black Code Laws were the extreme in racial profiling. These unconstitutional laws were purposely designed to dictate how the population of Americans of African descent could immigrate, or migrate, from one State, or city, to another within the United States. Because of these Black Code laws, and their impact on millions of African Americans, this population could not freely assimilate or integrate into the mainstream of society.

One must remember, at this point in our history, millions of African-Americans had neither a country nor a city to call their own. They were each legally declared to be three-fifths of a person and therefore did not merit federal or state constitutional privileges.

In order to understand the negative impulse behind the creation of the Black Code laws, one must understand the reasoning behind the cultural profiling within our immigration and naturalization policies. We must keep in mind that Southerners were entirely convinced by the status quo that African

> *Only two things are infinite, the universe and human stupidity, and I'm not sure about the former.*
>
> **Albert Einstein**

Americans were a present and fearful menace to white society. First, they feared the economic changes that would be brought on by allowing African Americans to assimilate into the workforce. Secondly, they feared that African-American males would intermingle with Caucasian women. Plainly, the principal motivation for the Black Codes was economic dominance.

Southerners were determined to bypass the 13th and 14th amendments and attempted to force the freed African Americans to work for them on their terms and conditions as they prescribed. They were determined to dominate the migration patterns of their ex-slaves, almost as completely as they had dominated them under the institution of slavery.

We believe that the men who passed these barbaric laws literally believed that they had to do something to preserve themselves, their families, and what was left of their fortunes after the Civil War. The Emancipation Proclamation would mean there would be a rising tide of African American refugees who were determined to compete for this nation's resources.

After the Civil War, the Radical Republicans advocated the passing of a comprehensive Civil Rights Bill. This legislation was purposely designed to protect African-Americans from the Black Code laws that the Southern States were planning to unleash. The launching of the Black Code laws was another way for the states to temporarily deny the Union the constitutional authority to abolish the sale of human beings as commodities.

Democratic President Andrew Johnson, in April 1866, vetoed the first Civil Rights Bill citing the Three-Fifths compromise agreement as already denying freed slaves of their civil liberties. Was he right? Bringing this first Civil Rights Bill onto the floor of Congress, at that moment in time, was an act of patriotism by the Radical Republicans. This act, if it had been passed, would have established a new era in our immigration, naturalization and commerce policies.

Backward Thinking Policies

The status quo's legal reasoning for our present day immigration and naturalization policies are backward thinking. These policies are lagging behind in the progress and development of a multi ethnic nation. It was not until 1964 that Democratic President Lyndon B. Johnson passed the Civil Rights Act.

The implementation of this Civil Rights Act had a far-reaching and a tremendous long-term impact on the immigration, naturalization and sexual orientation policies of the United States. It prohibited discrimination in public facilities, in government and in employment. It also invalidated both the Jim Crow and Black Code laws. However, there is no law that can be written that could alter the cultural mind-set of a spiteful person.

The unfairness of our immigration laws stem directly from the supremacy of the cultural common mind-set. These defective immigration and naturalization policies played a major role in the insincere and predictable treatment of Sonia Sotomayor, President Obama's choice for the Supreme Court. She was treated by some members of Congress, and the news media, as a second class citizen, as was President Obama.

> *"You cannot build character and courage by taking away a man's initiative and independence."*
>
> **Abraham Lincoln**

The Three-Fifths Compromise agreement was instrumental in establishing the immigration and naturalization policies of today. The intention of this compromise was to divide the people by their cultural beliefs and color. The objective was to control who could receive intergenerational transfer of wealth within the United States.

Those who are promoting the status quo want to keep the current immigration and naturalization policies in place. Politicians are presently using the illusion of race to legally determine a person's status within this country. Our immigration and naturalization policies are inconsistent and benefit only one segment of our society.

For over two hundred years our country's immigration and naturalization policies have been manipulated by our nation's elite. This manipulation continues to be the principle conflict and mistrust between the supremacy of a cultural common knowledge belief and scientific evidence.

Overriding Scientific Evidence

In the summer of 1875, the United States Courts commissioned scientists to gather scientific evidence that would prove to the world that the white European population in America was a separate race. What was discovered by the scientific commission was that the courts were wrong in their assessments about race. And that the European population of America was part of a sub-group of Caucasians that exists around the world. It was now scientifically proven that the white population of America is part of a larger group of people with different skin colors. There are Caucasians born with dark brown skin and blue eyes to pale or white skin and brown eyes.

Though the courts fundamentally, wanted to believe in the supremacy of a cultural common knowledge approach to governing and not in the scientific evidence. This permitted them to legally express the idea that their whiteness separated them from all other Caucasians groups. The court used their cultural common knowledge beliefs to override scientific evidence. It is this supremacy

Whoever undertakes to set himself up as a judge of Truth and Knowledge is shipwrecked by the laughter of the gods.

Albert Einstein

of a cultural common knowledge belief which established our National Census.

The United States Courts were disappointed with the findings of scientific evidence, which validated the fact that white skinned Americans did belong to the Caucasoid or Caucasian ethnic groups. The term *White* people should not be legally deemed as a race unto itself, as it exists presently on today's national census. These findings were not acceptable to the high courts. The supremacy of the cultural common knowledge approaches to immigration and naturalization policies were accepted.

It would have been heresy for the courts to admit to these findings of scientific evidence linking the white skin population to a sub-ethnic group within the Caucasian group itself. This type of evidence would have legally opened the doors to all Caucasians around the world attempting to legally gain citizenship.

These commissioned scientists were known as the "Commission for Scientific Racism". Their only purpose was to establish, through scientific methods, the differences between people based on their skin color. This commission's report was to support and validate the courts views of their beliefs of superior or inferior racial categories of other ethnic groups.

The supremacy of a cultural common knowledge belief and the illusions of race have created an enormous amount of human and social devastation. It has been revealed throughout this book that politicians who continue to use the phrase "playing the race card," are themselves delusional about race. They persist with their false beliefs in the face of strong contradictory scientific evidence, that there is but one race, and that is the human race.

The status quo continues to use the illusion of race in their pursuit for economic and social entitlements. They theorized that the cultural common knowledge approach to governing was the best legal method for controlling certain segments of the population. Prior to the ratification of The Fifth Amendment, only people who were recognized and legally declared to be white, and of the proper cultural beliefs, were allowed to become naturalized citizens of the United States. This racial illusion has restricted citizenship to non-Caucasian and other European Caucasian sub-groups such as Irish, Italians, Spaniards and Jews.

> *The best way to enhance freedom in other lands is to demonstrate here that our democratic system is worthy of emulation.*
>
> **Jimmy Carter**

Cultural Common Knowledge Approach

These court rulings used several analyses' for purposes of justifying the various racial divisions within our immigration and naturalization policies. This was done to allow their cultural common knowledge approach of governing to prevail. Previously, the courts were using two principle justifications for determining an individual's ethnic group. One was based on the appeal of the supremacy of cultural common knowledge approach to immigration and the other was based on scientific evidence.

This presented the courts with a constitutional dilemma, whether to adhere to the cultural common knowledge approach or the more realistic scientific evidence. Scientific evidence is based on universal scientific facts; whereas the supremacy of cultural common knowledge is based on one's cultural belief.

In the end, the supremacy of cultural common knowledge approach was chosen as the legal basis for immigration and naturalization policies, which are still in force today. The United States Supreme Court's decisions on immigration and naturalization policies have denied various members of our population their right to citizenship.

The courts used the cultural common knowledge belief to justify their determination that both Native Americans and Americans of African descent were not members of what was deemed to be the white race. The United States Supreme Court's rulings on immigration and naturalization policies were based on the Three-Fifths Compromise agreement and the presumption of one's cultural common knowledge beliefs.

The High Court's rejection of scientific evidence, and any other realistic deliberations regarding the authenticity of one's ethnicity, was out of fear and ignorance. The supremacy of a cultural common knowledge approach to immigration became the justification to deny naturalization to all ethnic groups who did not fit within the Court's cultural mind-set of the proper skin color

In 1909, the courts were split as to what was to be the proper standard in legally denying someone citizenship. The lower courts were divided. Six relied on the cultural common knowledge approach. Seven based their racial determinations on the scientific evidence suitability tests for a person's whiteness. In the two cases heard in 1922 and 1923, the Supreme Court broke the deadlock and ruled in favor of the supremacy of one's cultural common knowledge approach to immigration.

The Justices, who heard the fifty-two cases on racial qualification, were all Caucasian men. They controlled both the United States Supreme Court and the lower courts. Their rulings demonstrate that there is a great need for diversity within our courts and our Constitution. Racial determinations set the conditions for debates in the United States Supreme Court as to whether the supremacy of the cultural common knowledge approach to immigration would be acceptable in the future, as being constitutional.

What is Whiteness?

To the courts, whiteness was a social process created by a person's belief and their common outer features. The disagreement, with regard to using the whiteness test, surfaced more openly in cases where immigrants were from Western and Southeast Asia. Syrians, Asian Indians and other people with dark skin were scientifically classified as Caucasians by the leading anthropologists of that period.

As stated in *Ozawa v. United States*, the Supreme Court refused citizenship to a Japanese petitioner, holding that he was not of the type that was popularly known as the white race. The court quoted both the supremacy of cultural common knowledge and scientific evidence.

In these initial qualification cases, both scientific evidence and the popular supremacy of cultural common knowledge were used to bar all non-whites and certain other Caucasian applicants for United States citizenship. The Court refused to accept the scientific evidence, which it felt ignored the cultural and racial features, by including people with dark skin as being Caucasian. This was far more than what the bureaucrats who ran the courts could, or wanted, to envision.

> *"The distinction between the past, present and future is only a stubbornly persistent illusion.."*
>
> **Albert Einstein**

The United States Supreme Court viewed the scientific evidence on human differences to be a failure and a waste of the Courts time. The Court's theories of supremacy of cultural common knowledge approach to naturalization would become the cornerstone of American immigration laws.

The State's courts were now encouraged to make decisions based on a cultural common knowledge mind-set. It is the court's belief that people would use their common sense to discern who was white. The Court's disappointment with science was apparent and there was suspicion that the scientists were incapable of identifying what made up the white race. Being a part of the white population was the determining factor as to who could immigrate to this country.

The Court's frustrations with scientific evidence were understandable, because of anthropology's promising ability to definitively catalogue and determine the racial differences. This scientific theory of whiteness was a promise that science was unable to deliver. The Court rejected the failure of science to accomplish what it considered to be a simple task: to prove that whites in this country were separate from any other ethnic groups around the world.

This rejection of the scientific evidence by the Courts was the beginning of the Court's accepting the cultural common knowledge approach to immigration. The initial comparison between scientific evidence and the supremacy of cultural common knowledge failed to expose the inaccuracy of the United States Supreme Court's understanding of what makes up the white race. Scientific analysis has proven to the courts that there is no superior ethnic group.

Courts Reject Equality for Mankind

Not one of the courts wanted to depend on any scientific evidence that did not justify their unconstitutional racial assignments. This demonstrates that racial categorization does not depend solely on one's skin color. The supremacy of cultural common knowledge belief emerged as the only acceptable, or workable, racial examination that would be approved by the courts.

The supremacy of the cultural common knowledge belief is measured in terms of what the status quo wanted the population to believe. This theory of the supremacy of cultural common knowledge is still socially accepted today.

The social structure of the status quo is apparent in the court's denial of science and the induction of the supremacy of cultural common knowledge. It is this legal racial gauge of whiteness that was used to determine who could become a citizen of the United States. What if we discovered that our basic assumptions about race are wrong? What if people can be divided biologically along ethnic lines and not by the illusion of race or color?

If race is a biological myth; where did it originate? Why do our legislators continue to give race social standing and power? Did these assumptions begin with the Three-Fifths Compromise agreement? We must scrutinize this idea of racial assignments within our immigration and naturalization policies through the use of science.

> *"All that is valuable in human society depends upon the opportunity for development accorded the individual."*
>
> **Albert Einstein**

The High Court was confident that the supremacy of cultural common knowledge approach to immigration was constitutional. Some two hundred years later, the cultural common knowledge approach to immigration has proven to be an unreasonable system of laws. This cultural battle over immigration has become the center point of our lives. It is this hypothesis of the illusion of race that should be among our most fundamental discussions when it comes to improving poverty and education.

The Word Racism is Illusionary

Anthropologists, biologists and geneticists have established that there is only one race; the human race. If scientific analysis has proven there is only one race, then the courts have been incorrect in making the white skin color a race unto itself. Modern science continues to decode the genetic mysteries of DNA and has made the discovery that skin color is only skin deep.

However, the illusion of race is deeply embedded within the fabric of our Constitution, and within the hearts of men. We must investigate the latest in scientific breakthroughs to consti-tutionally eliminate the legal ramifications of the cultural com-mon knowledge belief within our immigration policies. People, desiring to come to this country, should not be legally or morally packaged into separate groups of races or colors. Yet, cultural profiling is incorporated into the immigration policies of our country.

The United States Supreme Court, and those in Congress at the time, believed in the theory of cultural common knowledge approach to immigration. This approach facilitated the creation of the Naturalization Act of 1790. This new immigration law limited citizenship to free Caucasian men only.

Ozawa, a Japanese immigrant and a former student of the University of California, appealed the rejection of his citizen-ship application in 1915. His argument was based on three points: 1) his skin was white, 2) that race should not be considered, and 3) he also believed in the supremacy of cultural common knowledge. Yet, the Supreme Court de-nied Ozawa's appeal, ruling that his skin may be white, but he was not Caucasian. And according to their cul-tural common knowledge beliefs, his skin was not white enough.

Several months after the Ozawa case, Bhagat Singh Thind, a South Asian immi-grant and U.S. Army veteran, petitioned for citizenship

> "A nation that is afraid to let its people judge the truth and falsehood in an open market is a nation that is afraid of its people."
>
> **John F. Kennedy**

> "All mankind is divided into three classes: those that are immovable, those that are movable, and those that move."
>
> **Benjamin Franklin**

presenting evidence that scientists classified East Indians as Caucasians. The court refuted its reasoning, as used in the Ozawa case, and ruled that Thind may be Caucasian, but he was not white, therefore his petition was denied.

The Courts argument against Thind's petition was that he had to be both Caucasian and have the whiteness of skin to be classified for citizenship under the Naturalization Act of 1795. In these two rulings, the Court has determined that people, who perceive themselves to be white, cannot legally consider themselves to be Caucasians. As a result of these decisions, the court has demonstrated, without a doubt, that our immigration policies are inconsistent and incoherent.

These inconsistent immigration policies gave Caucasian European Americans the opportunities and the advantages of both economic wealth and upward mobility. These economic opportunities are still being denied to millions of non-Caucasian Americans.

Reaping the Advantages of Whiteness.

There were other Caucasian groups within this country that were considered by the Supreme Court "not to be quite white". Among these were the Italians, the Jews and the Irish. Though in the end, they blended together with other Caucasians in America and reaped the advantages of their whiteness.

> "Most of the fundamental ideas of science are essentially simple, and may, as a rule, be expressed in a language comprehensible to everyone."
>
> **Albert Einstein**

Of the $120 billion that went into housing development, and was underwritten by the federal government between 1932 and 1964, less than 2% went to non-Caucasians. This is why, presently, the net worth of the average Non-Caucasian American family is about 1/8 that of the average Caucasian American family.

The majority of a Caucasian family's net worth is presently derived from the value of the family's estate. The estate process is called intergenerational transfer of wealth. It is the passing of the family estate from generation to generation.

> "The U. S. Constitution doesn't guarantee happiness, only the pursuit of it. You have to catch up with it yourself."
>
> **Benjamin Franklin**

The homes in neighborhoods that are predominantly Caucasian American sell for far more than those located in non-Caucasian neighborhoods. Therefore, their political power, their wealth, and any other advantages, or lack thereof, are being passed from one generation to the next. The availability for intergenerational transfer of wealth for each generation depends on one's ethnicity. Because of the compromise provision, ninety-five percent of Americans of African descent economically start at different points on the economic scale.

As we have said throughout this book, the source of all our immigration problems stem directly from The Three-Fifths Compromise agreement. This agreement is the deception of economic entitlement used by the status quo to control ninety-five percent of American's wealth

The illusion of race is so ingrained into our constitutional rule of law, and in the minds of men, that it has infected our national spirit to the point that most Americans cannot, or will not, grasp the crisis at hand. The illusion of race is fundamentally a part of our American society, as is our immigration policies. The effects of the illusion of race are being felt throughout our institutions and have blinded some Americans into believing that one race is better than another. Yet, just as individual's can act in racist ways, so have our nation's institutions.

Our immigration and naturalization policies have proven that the elite, with their hold on this nation's power, have continued to blind Americans for two centuries over the issues of race. Those who are privileged would like for us to believe that the major difficulties in our country are based on race. This is due to their preoccupation with racial dominance. However, this focus on race domination has done nothing for the majority of Americans.

Within this chapter we have done our best to illustrate to you how the elite utilize the illusion of race to control the wealth and power of this nation. This deception of race is a hoax. It has been perpetrated on the American people by those who inappropriately use the Three-Fifths Compromise agreement, and the immigration and naturalization policies, for their personal gain. We have written this chapter to put an end to this constitutional deception.

The main obstacle to equality in this country are these illusions of race, and the false misconceptions about skin color. The Founding Fathers were given the gift of wisdom and foresight for writing and framing the Constitution of the United of States with words that have given hope to generations. Now, it is upon our shoulders to complete the job that they started.

THE CANCER
FROM WITHIN

The Cancer from Within will expose three types of White Collar Crimes that are presently bankrupting our country. The first of these crimes is called Constitutional White Collar Crime. These crimes are the flawed passages written within the Article's of the Constitution.

The purpose for these constitutional crimes and the fraudulent language they contain are to withhold a person's economic chance for intergenerational transfer of wealth. These crimes of deception hinder the victim's chances to utilize the economic resources embedded within the Commerce Clause.

The first of these constitutional white collar crimes is the Three-Fifths Compromise agreement. It is this constitutional conspiracy that allows policymakers to unlawfully control commerce. This compromise provision was designed to secure the intergenerational transfer of wealth of the perpetrators to their descendents.

The second of these white collar crimes are what we call Governmental White Collar Crimes. These crimes are perpetrated by legislators and government employees. These crimes include those that were perpetrated by President's Abraham Lincoln and

Andrew Johnson. The last of these white collar crimes are committed within the private sector. The opportunities for committing the crimes of fraud, bribery, insider trading, embezzlement, identity theft and forgeries are more accessible to government employees, than they are within the private sector.

The term 'white-collar crime' dates back to 1939. This term was coined by Professor Edwin Hardin Sutherland. He theorized that white-collar criminals have different characteristics and motives than the typical street criminal. Professor Sutherland originally presented his theory on those crimes committed by high society to the American Sociological Society. He defined his ideas of white collar crime as, "crimes committed by persons of respectability and high social status in the course of their occupations". Though in reality, these acts of white collar crimes date back to 1787 with the insertion of the Three-Fifths Compromise agreement into the Constitution.

The principle goal of this compromise provision was to insure the future denial of basic liberty and economic wealth to the non-Caucasian population, as well as to women. This compromise provision embodies the essence of a constitutional miscalculation. This chapter will identify and define constitutional and governmental white collar crimes as illegal acts, or a series of illegal acts, that are committed by non- physical means for the purposes of deception and concealment by policymakers and bureaucrats.

> "If the people cannot trust their government to do the job for which it exists - to protect them and to promote their common welfare all else is lost."
>
> **Barack Obama**

Governmental crimes are commonly referred to as Public Corruption. These are breaches of the public's trust and an abuse of their position. Federal, state and local government officials have accomplices within the private sector. The Federal Bureau of Investigation has never debated, nor investigated, the economic impact that constitutional white collar crimes have on the country as a whole. In the private sector the victimizers pay penalties, while the victims may either lose small amounts of money or gain restitution.

The economic impact of constitutional and governmental white collar crimes on America has become self evident. There is little comprehension of the outward rippling effects that constitutional or governmental white collar crimes have on the elderly and the poor.

These crimes affect millions of people at the time of their commission and are felt for years, and in many cases, from one generation to the next. It is very difficult for the victims of governmental or constitutional crimes to gather the resources necessary to receive justice within the courts.

It is astonishing that a huge number of constitutional and governmental white collar crimes are committed against the elderly and the underprivileged. They too, have something to lose. Unlike the established middle class, the assets that are in jeopardy are all that stand between them and utter poverty. These types of crimes hinder the victim's only chance for creating wealth for themselves and their families. These crimes also hinder the ability to establish intergenerational transfer of wealth. The transferring of wealth is the next generation's capital, which will enable them to build their future economic security.

This chapter has established the Three-Fifths Compromise agreement as the vehicle that permitted the existence of constitutional and governmental white collar crimes. Americans need to become aware of the true economic conspiracies behind the formation of these crimes. This compromise provision is a powerful deception that uses Article One of the Constitution to hide its true intention.

The victims of constitutional and governmental white collar crimes are of all ages, ethnicity and sex. The offenders may be: lawmakers, judges, bureaucrats, bankers and yes, even religious leaders. These crimes, in many cases, forced some victims to surrender both their birthright and their name. These crimes are part of the Three-Fifths compromise conspiracy to deprive its victims of their Due Process of Law.

Constitutional and governmental white collar crimes are being felt throughout our socioeconomic system. The economic and emotional effects of these crimes are at epidemic levels and are ingrained into our system of laws. These types of crimes have infected our national spirit. They have economically exposed the middle class, and the underprivileged, to undue economic hardships.

> Most of the energy of political work is devoted to correcting the effects of mismanagement of government."
>
> **Milton Friedman**

The Three-Fifths Compromise agreement is a constitutional crime and is the direct result of the calculated efforts by legislators to keep the citizens ignorant of their hidden agendas. As Americans, we have failed to make the connection between the actual purpose of the Three-Fifths Compromise and the hijacking of our nation's wealth. Politicians continue to use the language within the compromise provision as a legal weapon to keep from sharing the wealth of our nation. Presently, this

> "Wherever there is interest and power to do wrong, wrong will generally be done."
>
> **James Madison**

compromise provision is responsible for unleashing the worst economic downturn in U.S. history.

The Hidden Agenda of the Compromise

The Three-Fifths Compromise is a constitutional failure. Its language and nature are entrenched within our tax laws and interfere with our voting rights. It also places an unjustifiable burden on the middle class, requiring them to pay taxes for the poor and the wealthy.

> *"Where an excess of power prevails, property of no sort is duly respected. No man is safe in his opinions, his person, his faculties, or his possessions."*
>
> **James Madison**

This compromise provision places millions of Americans at a disadvantage economically, making these unfortunate citizens 'indentured servants'. It also forces following generations of the poor to continue their parents lead into servitude, without any hope for economic change. The principle goal of the Three-Fifths Compromise agreement was to insure the denial of basic liberty and economic wealth to certain segments of the population.

Another reason the Founders inserted the Three-Fifths Compromise into the Constitution was to avoid utilizing the word 'slavery'. The Framers deliberately placed this compromise provision into Article One of the Constitution. They believed that it would legally shelter them from the economic crime of human exploitation. Yet they also believed and hoped that this intentionally corrupt provision would be corrected by a later Congress.

The Founders understood that the payment of restitution for the constitutional crime of slavery would have devastating economic implications for themselves and our nation. When it comes to the constitutional question of paying restitution for slavery's past, politicians today have the same fears exhibited by past Congresses. First of all, most, if not all, politicians fear the psychological and the economic cost of restitution. They also fear that if Congress were to grant restitution, it would cause a shift in the balance of power in America.

The status quo/politicians would lose significant control over the agencies of Immigration, and Commerce. The politicians would thereby lose control of over 95% of the population's resources. That is why Congress refuses to pay any form of restitution for this nation's crime against humanity. For Congress to continue their refusal to pay restitution for the constitutional crimes of slavery and the Three-Fifths Compromise, is itself, a form of constitutional enslavement.

This particular crime, the Three-Fifths Compromise, is embedded within Article One, Section Two, Paragraph Three of the Constitution. The language of the compromise is in total opposition to the true meaning of constitutional privileges. This compromise provision conceals the legal facts that permit the individual states to constitutionally take economic advantage of a particular segment of the population.

The Founding Fathers view of who should be privileged to receive the American dream was flawed. They based that judgment upon the cultural common knowledge approach to governing. This approach to governing is cultural profiling. In their haste to ratify the Constitution, they inserted this compromise provision and unknowingly opened a Pandora's Box to economic despair.

The Second Constitutional Crime.

The *second* of these constitutional crimes is Article One, Section Nine, Paragraph One, which states the "Powers Prohibited to Congress". This article prohibited Congress from enacting any laws that would regulate, or stop, the immoral and illegal act of migration, or importation, of slaves. This act was constitutionally enforced from 1787, until 1808.

The Powers Prohibited to Congress Act is a constitutional denial of basic Human

> *"America did not invent human rights. In a very real sense human rights invented America."*
>
> **Jimmy Carter**

Rights. The foundational language that makes up this act is fraudulent and deceptive. Powers Prohibited to Congress was purposely designed by policymakers of the time, to take advantage of the commerce clause which regulated the slave trade in America. This Act also placed an importation tax of ten dollars on each slave imported by the Southern states. The Federal Government's profit from this act of taxation was approximately one hundred and sixty million dollars in revenue.

The Powers Prohibited to Congress clause permitted the Federal Government to place a price tag on human lives. The policymakers of the time identified the victims of this constitutional crime to be nothing more than commodities. The Powers Prohibited to Congress clause makes parts of Article One dysfunctional. The fact that these Constitutional White Collar Crimes occurred more than two hundred years ago, should not hinder their correction.

Governmental White Collar Crimes

So far, within this chapter we have demonstrated two constitutional white collar crimes. Now, let us turn our attention to what we deem to be two Governmental White Collar Crimes. The first of these crimes was the *District of Columbia Emancipation Act,* signed April 16, 1862, by President Abraham Lincoln. The *District of Columbia Emancipation Act* entitled Washington

D. C. slave owners to be compensated a maximum of three hundred dollars for each American African slave who would later be emancipated. These former slaves were then offered one hundred dollars each, to join the overseas colonization plan, which would prove to be too costly.

> *"The people are the only legitimate fountain of power, and it is from them that the constitutional charter, under which the several branches of government hold their power, is derived."*
>
> **James Madison**

The Federal Government spent over a million dollars in purchasing approximately 3,100 slaves in their attempt to forcibly remove them to another country. *The District of Columbia Emancipation Act* was enacted nine months prior to the now famous "Emancipation Proclamation Address". This is the first recorded evidence that demonstrates that the Federal Government used tax dollars to re-purchase slaves. However, there are no records of the Federal Government ever paying monies to the newly purchased African refugees. The true purpose for the District of Columbia Emancipation Act was to exploit, and

> *There are risks and costs to action. But they are far less than the long range risks of comfortable inaction."*
>
> **John F. Kennedy**

then to export, these slave/refugees from our nation. The District of Columbia Emancipation Act is a deceitful and fraudulent crime, which economically rewarded the slave owners for their victimization of human beings.

Second of These Governmental Crimes

On March 3, 1865, right after the Emancipation Proclamation Act, President Lincoln signed the executive order creating the Bureau of Refugees, Freedmen and Abandoned Lands Act. This Act would economically assist the newly freed slaves to help them assimilate into the main stream of society.

This executive order allocated approximately two million acres of land for the settlement of African American families. The order included part of the island of Charleston, South Carolina, the abandoned rice fields along the river for thirty miles inland from the sea and the county's bordering the St. Johns River in Florida.

This was the first attempt by a Republican President and a Republican Congress to establish reparation, or restitution, to the African refugees for their military service. The military processed 400,000 acres of land, of the two million acres, into plots and the titles distributed to the heads of approximately 40,000 families of Americans of African descent. However, within months of taking office, President *Andrew Johnson*, a Southern Democrat, later confiscated these lands under the premise that the African race did not deserve a pathway to assimilation.

If this first attempt to compensate Americans of African descent for their military service had succeeded, it would have greatly benefited this deprived and impoverished population economically. Millions of African American families would have assimilated and integrated into the main stream of society. These estates, that were confiscated, would have created intergenerational transfer of wealth among the former African slaves and their descendants. Out of the two million acres of land that President Andrew Johnson confiscated, it was only "one percent" of the two hundred and eighty four million acres already held by Caucasian Americans.

How Did These Crimes Materialize?
We want to be fair-minded with regard as to how and why both of these Governmental White Collar Crimes were allowed to materialize. First of all, both Presidents Abraham Lincoln

and Andrew Johnson had sworn to preserve, protect and defend the Constitution. This is the mandated duty of any elected President. Their legal decisions to deny a people their human rights were based on the fraudulent language of the Three-Fifths Compromise agreement.

This compromise provision provided both Presidents with the constitutional authority to identify Africans as "others" to be treated as three-fifths of a population. As immoral as this may sound, our Constitution, because of this compromise provision, does not have the legal authority to protect those deemed to be three-fifths of a person. Therefore, both Presidents felt they were constitutionally and legally right in their decision for treating others inhumanely.

There is also a moral side to this equation, which questions the ethics of both men, since both committed crimes against humanity. What should happen when a seated United States President commits crimes against humanity? Is it the constitutional responsibility of the following generations to correct these wrongs? And how is it possible for any nation to place a price tag on crimes against humanity? The question remains, can our Constitution, which still contains this fraudulent agreement, correct these wrongs of injustice? The legal answer to this question would be, no.

> "The rights of persons, and the rights of property, are the objects, for the protection of which Government was instituted."
>
> **James Madison**

> "Human kindness has never weakened the stamina or softened the fiber of a free people. A nation does not have to be cruel to be tough".
>
> **Franklin D. Roosevelt**

The Three-Fifths Compromise agreement is the corrupt element established within the framing of the Constitution. It alone has corrupted the original fundamental principles to the concept of liberty. This miscalculation of judgment by the Founding Fathers allowed this compromise provision to be inserted into the Constitution. It was their first, but not last, shameful and dishonored error in judgment. Even with these errors, the essence and the core values of our Constitution remain sound. It is inevitable that an amendment to correct this compromise provision will help in the development of a fair and balanced society

We must face the fact that this compromise provision is a concealed weapon of deception committed by past legislators in the line of duty. It is an unlawful and unique agreement that is both structured and organized into our complex legal system to project the illusion of fairness.

This illusion of fairness has significantly affected how the Supreme Court of the United States conducts itself presently. So much so that in 1857, the court issued an order of cease and desist in cases that would be viewed as corruption by government officials. It is these desist and cease orders by the court, which placed government officials above the law.

The Federal Bureau of Investigation must adopt a wider approach in its investigations of white collar crimes. They should include constitutional and governmental white collar crime within their list of capital crimes. Individuals such as legislators who attempt to

> *"No government can help the destinies of people who insist in putting sectional and class consciousness ahead of general weal."*
>
> **Franklin D. Roosevelt**

commit, or actually do commit, governmental fraud should be prosecuted to the fullest extent of the law, just as any low level white collar criminal.

The Federal Bureau of Investigation does not include in their investigations the socioeconomic crimes perpetrated on people living in ghettos. They must scrutinize the relationship of socioeconomic and constitutional white collar crimes on society as a whole.

The debate on what qualifies as white-collar crime needs to be expanded to constitutional and governmental white collar crimes. The terminology on governmental white collar crime encompasses a variety of nonviolent actions, usually committed for financial gain by government officials. Perpetrators of governmental white collar crimes use a sophisticated series of complex transactions to conceal their activities, which makes for a difficult prosecution.

Tax Fraud and Embezzlement

The language of the Three-Fifths Compromise agreement has the same fraudulent elements of common white-collar crimes. These elements include anti-trust violations, tax, healthcare fraud and embezzlements. The Federal Bureau of Investigation estimates the costs of common white-collar crimes within the United States to be more than $300 billion dollars annually. But, the true costs of constitutional and governmental white collar crimes cannot be quantified.

The cost of these crimes affect mostly the elderly and the poor. Constitutional and governmental white collar crimes do not prompt public outrage or draw the lengthy prison sentences, as do recipients of the welfare system, who sign affidavits swearing to report their income. Governmental white collar criminals, in areas like the pharmaceutical and health insurance industries, are economically devastating our country's finances. These governmental crimes are having a major impact on the country's health care decisions. The pharmaceutical and health care insurance companies are perpetrating these crimes on American citizens by way of Congress' approval.

The fraudulent languages of this compromise provision must be set aside in order to end the looting of America's wealth. After writing and crafting the Three-Fifths Compromise agreement, our Founding Fathers recognized that this compromise provision would make part of the Constitution a deceptive document.

The economic and psychological impact of The Three-Fifths Compromise on this nation, and its people, is far more economically devastating than our Founding Fathers anticipated. Most of our political and commerce difficulties may be traced to this compromise provision. There are no statistics to show the percentage of Americans who have experienced some form of victimization by these governmental crimes during their lifetime

Private Sector White Collar Crimes'

Our Founding Fathers could not comprehend the dreadful economic side effects that the Three-Fifths Compromise would have on America's social economy. To some degree they flattered themselves about this compromise provision, as if the act was representative of the whole human race. They had no idea that this nation would itself be economically defrauded by the boomerang effects of this unconstitutional act.

The last of these white collar crimes are those committed within the private sector. It must also be understood that white collar crimes are also committed by people within the lower income status as well. Their actions also harm our economy.

Here are some examples of the private sector engaging in white-collar crime activities: filing false income tax returns, fraudulent claims for social security benefits, concealing assets in a personal bankruptcy and the use of

> *Government's first duty is to protect the people, not run their lives.*
>
> **Ronald Reagan**

large-scale buying on credit with no intention of ever paying for those purchases. Regardless, if it is constitutional, governmental or the private sector, white collar crimes are economically devastating to our society. With all the facts and years of examining the Three-Fifths Compromise provisional language; it still seems like an old fashioned con game on the American people. This unconstitutional act has backfired and is now affecting every American.

White collar crimes can also be committed by persons who operate poverty programs and are authorized to hire a work group and instead place fictional workers on the payroll. They do this so they can appropriate these fictional workers wages. These types of governmental white collar crime are done every day in this nation. Even city and state officials are stealing billions of your tax dollars each year from the different types of welfare programs.

We know a double standard has been built into our Constitution, and our law enforcement structures, to allow this form of governmental crime to exist. It is important that we have deterrence through investigations, evaluations and prosecutions with stricter sentencing of the violators.

Our policymakers have established a unique legal structure with complex proceedings, injunctions and desist and cease orders. This was done to hide common law frauds when committed in a business, government or constitutional context. Whereas, less sophisticated thieves, who are poor or middle class, must face additional criminal charges for committing similar acts in the course of their brief and less lucrative activity. While the same crime committed in a business or governmental context, the victimizer would get no more than a slap on the wrist or be given immunity for their violations.

White Collar Crime on Main Street

Banks deliberately take risks, by mailing unsolicited credit cards to the disadvantaged. They relegate the possible fraud losses, to the cost of doing business, knowing full well; the tax payers will bail them out. As individuals we are exposed to constitutional and governmental white collar crime more than any other crime.

We are more likely to deal with strangers over the phone than deal with those we know and whose blemishes we can assess. We are more exposed now than ever before. We tend to depend, not on one another but; on lawmakers, computers and the Federal Government.

All consumers rely on the weights and measures as marked, when we make purchases of prepackaged merchandise or foods. We cannot check if the measurements are correct. We refuse to believe that government food inspectors would permit undesirable portions of any animal to be used as ground meat for our hamburger. We are shocked when we hear of sporadic investigations disclosing things that are not right with our food. These crimes are done in the name of greed.

What are Major and Minor Offences?

Constitutional and Governmental white collar crimes are of low visibility and have a high impact on our society. These crimes are easily committed and covered-up, because of the fraudulent nature of our economic organizations within our government oversight.

The new scams in marketing, distribution, and investment banking on Wall Street are creating waves upon waves of fraudulent acts. Governmental white-collar crime also weighs heavily on the elderly of our society. Seniors are being separated from their homes, their communities and their children. The increased complexity of our society heightens their vulnerability because of the increased difficulty in obtaining justice for their losses and suffering.

Legal services are costly, prosecutors and investigators are overburdened, and court calendars are clogged. Victims of white collar crimes, regardless of the type, must consider the time it takes to obtain compensation. The victims sometime wonder whether they will be the major sufferers or the targets of their complaint. Constitutional and governmental white collar crimes, along with the fines, must be raised to levels which realistically punish the victimizer

> *"The test of our progress is not whether we add more to the abundance of those who have much it is whether we provide enough for those who have little. "*
>
> **Franklin D. Roosevelt**

No dollar amount can adequately identify the costs of constitutional and governmental white-collar crime on the American people. How does one set dollar values on civil rights violations or food and drug violations? These crimes can permanently and economically disable, or even kill.

There are companies, without valid deposit insurance, which destroy the life savings of the elderly and can make them a burden on their children or on the state. A more concerned analysis will

> *Anyone who doesn't take truth seriously in small matters cannot be trusted in large ones either.*
>
> **Albert Einstein**

show that the impact of such crimes is on the people, and their physical and psychological integrity. Constitutional and governmental white collar crime is not like a common crime, but it has a serious influence on the fabric of our society, and on the freedoms of commercial and interpersonal transactions.

We should take special note of the impact of constitutional and governmental white collar crimes on Non-Caucasians, women, the elderly and the poor. This includes people who are trapped in ghettoes or rural areas because of these crimes. The very poor, and particularly the destitute elderly, are profitable targets for those engaged in governmental white-collar crime activities.

Although, in the private sector, if a mother is shorted on the food she buys with her food stamps, the impact on her family is clear. The true and ultimate vulnerability for the poor is that their possessions or assets will be lost forever, and they cannot afford to get them back.

In some instances, the victims lack of knowledge makes the fraud almost a certainty because of the context in which the wrongful actions arise. Sometimes ignorance of the facts is inevitable in the face of a calculated effort to mislead people. However, the efforts to deceive and mislead are only too often matched by carelessness or greediness of the victim. It does little good to require a brief to be issued in connection with the sale of stocks or a home, if the purchaser will not read the fine print.

This isn't so with the crime of the Three-Fifths Compromise agreement. This crime was constitutionally forced upon Americans. It has been hidden in plain view and has been economically defrauding Americans for hundreds of years. It's hard to imagine a way out from under the grips of governmental and constitutional white collar crimes. These crimes have forced millions of Americans into some form of welfare.

This chapter, "The Cancer From Within", lays out the legal tools Americans needs to begin the task of protecting their income. This includes suggestions for personal and collective actions that make a difference, as well as, realistic, concrete solutions to some of the most difficult economic challenges facing our nation today.

There are many ways you can protect yourself from the Cancer From Within. The remedies that are needed to overcome these crimes are within the noble parts of the Constitution itself. It is our hope that this chapter will provide you and your families with the knowledge, the know-how and the inspiration to stand fast against these forms of white collar crimes.

7

IRREVERSIBLE DAMAGE:
WHAT IS YOUR NAME?

There is a form of abduction occurring within our society that has been mysteriously and constitutionally hidden. It is buried deep within the frameworks of our legal systems. This abduction is both a spiritual and a legal raping of one's culture, birthright and civil liberties.

> "A nation that is afraid to let its people judge the truth and falsehood in an open market is a nation that is afraid of its people."
>
> **John F. Kennedy**

The victims of this abduction are being forced to accept slave names at birth, and their descendents will be branded with the names of slavery's past for generations to follow. The abduction of a person's birthright is just as difficult from which to recover; as are the emotional side effects of slavery itself.

Being branded with a slave name is hard to imagine, especially since the victims of these crimes are Americans. The abduction of one's heritage is not a new phenomenon in this country. It has been constitutionally hidden to strip away a person's humanity. This abduction, not only negatively affects the victims; it also affects our nation's economic resources.

This chapter provides an overview of the key differences between a slave name and one's true birthright. Most victims of this abduction are being forced to identify with characteristics that are European. Explanations will also be given as to why the structures of our names are such powerful symbols on one's outlook of life. The commandeering of a person's ancestral name places a needless economic, and psychological burden on the victim's self-worth.

As in most countries, it is customary that a person inherit their father's name at birth. Whereas, when one is the descendant of an African American slave; your father's ancestral name, which was to be naturally handed down to you, has been constitutionally eradicated.

These acts of abduction have constitutionally and spiritually; allowed for the victims of these abductions to become bastards, in name only. This means that the victims of these abductions were denied the privilege of receiving their father's ancestral name, as if their fathers legacies never existed.

> "The great enemy of the truth is very often not the lie, deliberate, contrived and dishonest, but the myth, persistent, persuasive and unrealistic."
>
> **John F. Kennedy**

The European names the victims of these abductions received are illegitimate. They are deceptive and an emotional burden on these Americans. The victims of these abductions do not have an accurate impression of their history because of their deceptive names. Their past history has been suppressed, distorted and destroyed for cultural and economic reasons.

Other ethnic groups in this nation enjoy the privilege of being born with their true name/birthright. Americans of African descent have not been accorded this privilege. The majority of these victims are not even aware of these violations, and the sub-conscious grief it has on their psyche.

This chapter, "Irreversible Damage: What is Your Name", is written for the victims of these unthinkable acts. The purpose of this chapter is to help the victims understand this constitutional abduction and how it has affected their lives. This will enable them to understand their internal shame, without placing fault on themselves or others.

We will explain the economical and psychological repercussions that have materialized because of these abductions. We will also demonstrate how the process of abduction occurred in this country in the first place. These abductions originated within the American slave industries. Also lawmakers/bureaucrats utilize the Three-Fifths Compromise agreement as a constitutional weapon for controlling the victim's wealth and their dignity.

This compromise provision facilitated the continuance of these abductions of people from their homelands, raping them of their freedom and their birthrights. The ill effects of these adductions,

> *"Without forgiveness, there's no future."*
>
> **Desmond Tutu**

which were established more than four hundred years ago, are still having a lasting and harmful effect on the victim's offspring. The significance of each person having their true heritage and honorable birthright will be illustrated.

We hope every citizen and victim of these hidden crimes will seize upon this new found knowledge and use it in a constructive way. Our main objective is to help guide the victims of these constitutional abductions to a place that they would come to understand the gravity of this situation. This new awareness, will give them the pathway to become victorious over their new given identities. There are many culprits to these legal abductions, but the principle one is the Three-Fifths Compromise agreement. This compromise was, and still is, an over- reaching, backward- thinking provision.

Americans of African descent are the only people born in the United States with the constitutional process of receiving a slave's name at birth. These names are transferred from one generation to the next, causing economic and psychological anguish, without the victim ever consciously being aware of its negative legal impact.

These slave re-naming polices make part of our constitutional rule of law defective in their application. In essence, these abductions are not only unconstitutional, but also immoral. It was made exceedingly clear by previous Congress' that the re-naming of the African slave population, and their descendants, was deemed to be legal and binding.

Both the foundation of our nation and the Constitution were founded on the backs of the victims of this crime of abduction. This process of abduction continues to test the moral fiber of this nation, and its people, and should not be allowed to persist in its present form. These abductions should be treated as constitutional crimes against humanity.

A New Perspective on Life

We intend to reveal what happens to an ethnic group's self esteem and their wealth, when their traditions and birthrights have been purposely eradicated. Within these pages you will encounter a new perspective on how a person's name forms one's intellect.

One's name also forms one's behavior. This includes things such as; being open-minded, stable, and being at peace with one's self. It is essential that this nation come to recognize a person's inner qualities develop naturally with their ancestral name.

The fundamental purpose of having an ancestral name is to develop harmony and relativity between one's mind, and one's inner potential. The fundamental purpose for renaming the African slaves was to destroy their self worth, through the humiliation and the loss of their heritage. This would strip them of any chance of future wealth.

It is this re-naming process that permitted the slave owners, and the status quo of the time, to psychologically and physically dominate their investments in human commodities. This re-naming process forced the African population to lose both their legacy and their personal history. These acts of abduction would insure the continuation of the intergenerational transfer of shame for an estimated 320 million Americans of African descent.

> *Always remember that others may hate you but those who hate you don't win unless you hate them. And then you destroy yourself*
>
> **Richard M. Nixon**

Your name is one of many keys to your success, and your first inheritance at birth. It is intergenerational and the legal process by which we are identified. Our name is our only true inheritance and our only real possession that must be defended by each succeeding generation. Our belief in the dignity of life stems directly from the faith in our name. Therefore, we must honor and take pride in our identity. As a nation, we must insure that these crimes of abduction never be permitted to happen again.

What is a Slave Name?

A Slave name is a name given to persons who have been enslaved, or a name inherited from enslaved ancestors. What if you were born with a slave name? How could you search for your real heritage? Can you make a distinction as to who you really are? Could you identify your true personality? How would you be able to inherit your wealth?

During the slavery experience, the forcing of a name change on the victims of slavery was meant to be derogatory, for purposes of their victimization. Upon emanci-

> *"Never be bullied into silence. Never allow yourself to be made a victim. Accept no one's definition of your life; define yourself."*
>
> **Harvey Fierstein**

pation, the slaves and their descendents, were known as freedmen. The freed slaves were required by law to identify themselves within those states from where they had been emancipated. They were unable to use their traditional African names since those names had been constitutionally erased.

Freedmen/former slaves were forced to use the names given to them by their owners. The only other names available were those of contemporary people of social importance, or historical figures. Some of these names are those of former presidents such as: Washington, Jefferson and Jackson.

Americans of African descent are the only ethnic group within our nation, who constitutionally suffer the weight of a slave identity. For another human to forcefully eradicate someone's name is clear evidence of their notion of supremacy. These Americans, whose ancestors were the primary victims of the re-naming process, have forever lost their birthrights, their true names, along with their legacy.

The same European names enjoyed by Caucasian Americans have become badges of shame for most Americans of African descent. My brother and I are prime examples of this badge of shame. It is possible that we inherited our name of Gates from the ancestors of Bill Gates, of Microsoft or Robert Gates, former Head of the U.S Defense Department.

There are many vast differences between the cultural characteristics of a European name and that of an African name. Some African Americans, including Cassius Clay and Lou Alcindor, changed their names. Cassius Clay changed his name to Mohammed Ali. Lou Alcindor changed his to Kareem Abdul Jabbar. They felt that their European names were spiritually enslaving them in slavery's past and they no longer desired to be a part of that era.

> *"For goodness sake, will they hear, will white people hear what we are trying to say? Please, all we are asking you to do is to recognize that we are humans, too."*
>
> **Desmond Tutu**

Other ethnic groups within our country have the privilege of their ancestral names, but not Americans of African descent. The perpetrators of the slave trade did not take into account, nor did they care about, the *irreversible* psychological and economic damage that would occur in our nation among their African captives.

The forcing of European names victimized the African population. This renaming policy has been a limiting factor to the victim's life and their future inheritance. Any other name, but one's true ancestral name, creates a degree of spiritual and mental tension. These abductions allow for the existence of hostility towards the perpetrators. A person's true name is essential to one's sound reasoning. This can never be overstated.

The slave trade subjected the African captives and their descendents to needless and severe limitations in their life choices. Because of these European names, the descendents of Americans of African descent have been denied the right to life, liberty and the pursuit of happiness.

More importantly, does the forceful removal of a person's birthright make them inferior or flawed? In some instances, yes! That was the slave owner's intention. One's name is how one identifies themselves and how others

> *"You can never solve a problem on the level on which it was created."*
>
> **Albert Einstein**

properly identify them. The African slaves who were brought to America were stripped of their ancestral heritage to give them new identities. This was done to control their sense of self-worth and any future wealth the slave, and their descendents, might generate.

The Hidden Power of a Name

Your name is a lifetime of shared thoughts and inspiration. It is the foundation of your conscious intelligence and your identity. It is you. Your ancestral name is the one true possession that connects you to your ancestors. An authentic birthright is what brings you the respect and the success you hope to achieve in life.

Your brain is a physical instrument, but it is not the foundation of your mind and spirit. The foundation of your mind and spirit is provided by the trustworthiness of your ancestral name. When an honorable name is given to an individual, there are undeniable specific spiritual forces at play. These forces, combined with one's conscious intelligence and spiritual beliefs are what give one a comprehensive outlook on life. This arrangement of conscious intelligence and your ancestral name launches the nucleus of one's mental characteristics and abilities. The authority of one's name brings to life that person's individuality.

Therefore, does having a slave name pre-dispose one's personality to be subject to the callousness of life? Do all names have meaning? Are Americans of African descent being treated differently because of their European slave names? The answer to all three of these questions is, yes. Research shows that a person's name makes both positive and negative impressions on a person's psyche. For example, Bill Gates, the founder of Microsoft, bears the image of a popular, self-assured person. My name is also Gates, but I am African American. My name bears the image of slavery's past.

Our research, along with my experience as a victim of these abductions, indicate that a person's self-worth is affected by their name, as much as by the behavior of others. Nevertheless, people unconsciously, but effectively, send negative messages to the victims of this abduction. I am the victim of my European name of Gates, but it is the only legal identity given to me at birth.

> *"Let us not seek the Republican answer or the Democratic answer, but the right answer. Let us not seek to fix the blame for the past. Let us accept our own responsibility for the future."*
>
> **John F. Kennedy**

Barrack Hussein Obama, 44th President of the United States, is bi-racial. His ethnicity is both that of European and African descent. However, because of the fraudulent language within the Three-Fifths Compromise agreement, the Jim Crow laws, and the immigration and naturalization policies, President Obama is constitutionally categorized as a black man, only!

The Three-Fifths Compromise provision deems President Obama to be three-fifths of a whole person, because of the ethnicity of his African side. President Obama is also biologically a Caucasian American on his mother's side. In accordance with previously enforced Black Code Laws and today's census, President Obama cannot legally declare himself to be a Caucasian American.

President Obama's mother was aware of the benefits to her son in keeping his ancestral birthright. Barack Hussein Obama was not born burdened with a slave name. Through his birth he acquired his ancestral birthright, which the majority of Americans of African descent can never take pleasure in.

The President acquired his name from his father, a free man from Africa. This permitted the intergenerational transfer of his birthright from his father to him. President Obama's children were both born free from the adverse affects of having a slave name. This spared his children from the pain of slavery's past.

This story on how President Barack Hussein Obama acquired his ancestral name demonstrates our theory that a true ancestral name can have a positive effect on your life. Is it possible that Barack Obama, Muhammad Ali and Kareem Abdul Jabbar achieved and established their successes because of a cultural name? Or was it the differences in languages and alphabetical symbols that had a distinctive consequence in the creation of their success in life?

There is a vast difference between the characteristics of the English language and those characteristics of African languages. Therefore, to avoid any adverse effects to one's spiritual reasoning and conscious intelligence, the proper language characteristics must be present at the time of one's birth.

The process of this abduction makes our Constitution's rule of law inadequate for one segment of our population. Every person who has an authentic birthright can look to their past, for answers, with an insight to their future.

The Importance of Your Ancestral Name

Why is it fundamentally important to know the value of your ancestral name? One's name is the foundation of the constructive qualities that form the processes of your thoughts. This is what makes up your individual personality. African Americans, by far, are the sole victims of this type of constitutional abduction in America.

The European names forced upon them do not provide the natural outlet of expression and developments for their inner purpose, nor does it establish their legal rights. Presently, because of these slave names, the only true heritage, or tradition, that the majority of Americans of African descent experience in this nation is rejection.

The fundamental nature of this abduction is the raping of an individual's self-worth. The purpose of these abductions are to seize control, through legal assaults, on the birthright of a certain segment of the population. This commandeering of the individual's inner self is a scar on the heart and soul of every African American with a slave name. One's name is a reflection of one's culture, the past, the ancestry, and also one's spirituality. Any separation from one's heritage will affect and interfere with your outlook on life.

The Effects of this Crime

When you are born your existence and your surroundings are influenced by your name. This is why a proper name is essential. Persons born with a slave name sometimes develop a degree of apprehension and hostility towards life. The victims of these abductions do not realize their European name is interfering with their inner-peace. For example; consider a radio station, which has constant static which interferes with your musical enjoyment, would you continue to listen, or would you change the station?

A slave name not only interferes with a person's self-worth, but it makes the victims of this abduction spiritually, economically and psychologically unbalanced. The effects of these abductions create a tension that is hidden deep within the victim's sub-conscious. Scientific evidence has shown that a person's name does have an effect on one's attitude, which also influences one's health. This abduction of one's name not only generates an unhealthy economic environment, but it is also harmful to the economic-wellness of America.

Because of these abductions, the victims sometimes feel embittered, angry or distrustful of others. Whether consciously or sub-consciously, these destructive thoughts will eventually become physical ailments. I believe that after four hundred years of these abductions, the victims have been overwhelmed and distressed by this process, without knowing it. Because of the distress of these abductions, this segment of the population has been sub-consciously and genetically afflicted with physical ailments such as high blood pressure.

> "Human rights is the soul of our foreign policy, because human rights is the very soul of our sense of nationhood."
>
> **Jimmy Carter**

There are some Americans of African descents who consciously blame the status quo for the loss of their birthright. The majority of Americans are not aware that Americans of African descent are affected economically and psychologically by the loss of their ancestral name.

Legally, Americans of African descent have no remedy for recovering their heritage or birthright. We must work together, as a nation, to resolve the psychological pain of this crime. As Americans, we must accept the facts that the Three-Fifths Compromise agreement, once again, is the victimizer of these abductions.

> "The purpose of separation of church and state is to keep forever from these shores the ceaseless strife that has soaked the soil of Europe with blood for centuries."
>
> **James Madison**

The issues of these abductions have, for many years, been purposely overlooked by our legislators. Americans of African descent ought to understand that their European names should no longer be a rejection of their humanity. These issues of abductions must be discussed throughout this nation to negate the effects that continue to influence how Americans of African descent identify themselves and their nation.

The majority of Americans have been blindsided by the hidden phenomena of these abductions. Once a person realizes that they have been a victim of this crime, they will be better equipped to decide whether to keep their European name or to change it.

As the author I, too, am a victim of this crime of abduction. Though I spiritually and emotionally refuse to accept this name as my birthright, I have no choice but to legally use it. The only reason I have not changed my slave name is because my ancestral name is forever lost.

My acceptance of this truth has been, and still is, a challenge. Certainly, I am fully aware that my European name, "Gates", binds my children and me to slavery's past. There is much more to these abductions that cannot be included within this chapter.

It will take many generations before this country can become reconciled to this crime against humanity. More importantly, how should Americans react to the shocking fact that a particular group of their country men and women are bound by a name of shame?

As a victim of this abduction, I have come to realize that the language and theories within our Constitution are likened to a "two edge sword". For the victims of this abduction, the defective language within the Three-Fifths Compromise has severed their ancestral history.

While the noble language within this Constitution has shielded the victims of this abduction, allowing them to receive wisdom, strength, honor, and the blessings of an honorable nation.

8

THE SOURCE OF HOPE
AND HONOR

"The Source of Hope and Honor", was written to convey to Americans how they can obtain their vision of becoming economically and psychologically sound, regardless of their ethnicity or cultural beliefs. Americans can accomplish their economic goals by taking advantage of the hidden financial and political tools within the Constitution.

There are two great divisions within our country. First, there is the Continental Divide, known as the Rocky Mountains, created by deity. Secondly, the supremacy of cultural common knowledge approaches to governing, created by man. This approach to governing was conceived by the elite to divide the people by color and their cultural beliefs. This is why, the Founding Fathers fashioned the Constitution with a functional purpose for compromise when necessary...

This document, our Constitution, is the inspiration of man. Most Articles are based on the supremacy of a cultural common knowledge belief, where religious rights supersede civil rights. Then, there are the Articles of Amendments. They are based on the fundamentals of the theory of true conservatism. These Amendments mainly focus on one's civil liberties.

The true purpose of our Constitution is to first benefit the states. Secondly, it was designed to protect the free will of its citizens. The Constitution reflects the Founders somewhat keen understanding of what they felt about humanity. They were also aware that this Constitution could be employed as a weapon in the wrong hands.

> "Don't go around saying the world owes you a living. The world owes you nothing. It was here first."
>
> **Mark Twain**

The Founders did make, as they feared, a few errors while writing the Constitution. They failed to allow for its normal transformation from an innocent document to a series of noble Articles. The Founding Fathers miscalculated the dreadful economic division and psychological effects the Three-Fifths Compromise agreement would have on the Union.

Any constitutional rule of law that is not productive, or is defective, will not bring honor or prosperity to its citizens or the states. In time, this compromise provision will make the Constitution worthless. Our Constitution's noble transformation will not be realized until we have learned, as a nation, to deal with the imperfections within ourselves and within our rule of law.

Imperfections in life and within the Constitution are a certainty. Imperfection is a part of humanity itself. This is why, it is necessary we learn to take full advantage of these constitutional errors Within this chapter, we will articulate four major visions for this nation. The objectives of these visions are to restore the source of *hope, honor,* and *wealth* within our society. The only way to accomplish these objectives is to take full advantage of the errors written within the Constitution, turning them into productive economic values.

The first of these visions is *Hopefulness,* where optimism and expectations of fairness are the rule. Secondly, there is the vision of our *Freedoms,* where protecting our religious and civil liberties are the driving forces of the American way of life. The third vision is becoming a more *Grateful Country,* where each generation of Americans is taught to appreciate the role that the federal government play's in their lives. Lastly, is the vision of becoming a *Pro-ethnic Society,* where multi-ethnicity is our American heritage.

It is imperative that our children are taught the seriousness of these visions. My siblings and I were taught by our parents to recognize the true value of these four innovative visions. We were taught that these visions were the building blocks for the theories of True Conservatism. We were also taught that the source of our wealth, hope and honor stem directly from the timeless, living and evolving words of the Constitution. Furthermore, we were taught not to let any challenge or individual hinder our visions in our pursuit for economic wellness.

> "Those who want the Government to regulate matters of the mind and spirit are like men who are so afraid of being murdered that they commit suicide to avoid assassination."
>
> **Harry S. Truman**

Most Americans experience life by sitting on the sidelines and waiting for things to happen. These types of people feel they can neither control, nor influence, their economic circumstances. As the author, I discovered in order to make economic change, or a difference in my environment, I would have to fully understand how our system of laws function in a business like setting.

I also realized that to become a multi-ethnic-society, it would be essential that we have common national and economic goals to achieve. Our *national goals* should be the protection of our constitutional way of life. Our *economic goals* should be to restore our nation's wealth. However, we must remember that wealth comes in many forms other than money

I have seen too many of my fellow Americans who have worked hard, paid their fair share in taxes and not advanced in their positions economically. These men and women are educated, but they do not know their constitutional rights or how to apply them in a business like fashion.

The Vision of Hopefulness

For the average American to become economically sound, one needs to understand a basic economic truth about wealth in this country. The status quo, for more than two hundred years, has been doing their best to keep this economic truth to themselves, making it their trade secret.

Presently, America is in an economic crisis, where Ninety-five percent of its citizens need to know how to employ this economic secret for their survival. This secret is not difficult to understand, it is part of the language within the Three-Fifths Compromise agreement, as well as, that of Commerce Clause.

The status quo appreciates and comprehends the powerful economic influence the Commerce Clause has on their business and their political positioning. They understand that to create wealth, one also needs a plan to maintain that wealth. By incorporating the language within the Commerce Clause, and that of the Three-Fifths-Compromise provision, they created an economic system called the trickledown effect.

Americans who desire to economically benefit from the secrets of the status quo must become educated in utilizing, and redesigning, the Commerce Clause. As guardians of the Constitution, we have the responsibility to teach these economic skills to the generations that follow. As a humble American whose life experiences are based on my expectations of fairness, it is the noble languages within our Constitution which helped me to improve my outlook on life.

Like most Americans, I did not appreciate, nor did I understand, the Constitution's rule of law, or its application. Therefore, I believed it to be the tool used by the politicians, Wall Street and those in the banking industry, for their success. It was my yearning for economic success which helped me look beyond this nation's past.

The longing to be free from our nation's past errors propelled me to move forward to my destiny. I came to accept the wrongs of the past, as just that, the past. I became a forward thinker when I discovered that I could not mend the past. This awareness allowed me to focus on the situation at hand, my economic future. This new found knowledge brought me closer to the objectives of my economic visions. These new possibilities renewed my aspirations for writing this book.

It is my desire, as the author, to let Americans know that we must stop looking back at our past and complaining. Looking back at our past errors, without the desire or means of correcting them, is troublesome at best. As a multi ethnic nation, we cannot allow this country to continue to lose its constitutional vision of liberty.

> *"If you don't design your own life plan, chances are you'll fall into someone else's plan. And guess what they have planned for you? Not much."*
>
> **Jim Rohn**

We must collectively work together to solve our nation's economic and cultural problems. Each of us has a destiny to fulfill in this country. It was my destiny to write this book in the hope of uniting our nation. Anyone who understands this nation's vital information, and has taken the time to learn from it, will be able to control their economic destiny. It's that simple.

The road to economic success will cost you nothing, but your time and hard work. Before I understood the constitutional rules for success, I would wonder how people became successful. One of those persons who is successful, and whom I admire, is Bill Gates, of Microsoft. I asked myself "why was he so successful, how did he come by it, and how could I acquire it?"

Then I began to visualize some possible answers to my questions, such as, is he successful because he has the political correct color? Was his business successful because he was born into money, or is it because he attended better schools?

As I reflected on my answers, it became obvious to me that it was not just his education that made him successful. Nor was it about his political connections. It was primarily his faith in himself and his belief in his country. Also, it was his understanding of the legal system, and his love for technology that allowed him to generate his wealth. The most important lesson for me about Bill Gates' road to success was: what do I need to make myself successful?

One day, as I visited a book store, I came upon a book entitled, "Business, the Speed of Thought: Using a Digital Nervous System". This book was written in part by Bill Gates. As I read this book, it demonstrated to me that Bill Gates' success was mostly due to his acquiring the right information, which helped him secure the future of his business.

> "No one has been barred on account of his race from fighting or dying for America, there are no white or colored signs on the foxholes or graveyards of battle."
>
> **John F. Kennedy**

Similar to Bill Gates I, too, acquired some important business information early in my life. I learned how to becoming a realist, a forward thinker. My biggest hurdle was grasping the fact that not every person in this country is being treated equally. However, no obstacles should hold a person back from going after his or her goals in life. Once I understood this fact, I became proactive with my life, and saw the best in others. This allowed me to accept, as true; that there is nothing in this world that can prevent me from reaching my full potential.

> "Learn from yesterday, live for today, hope for tomorrow. The important thing is not to stop questioning."
>
> **Albert Einstein**

There are two things that I have in common with Bill Gates. First, we share family names. Secondly, we share the belief and a respect for our nation's future. No matter which side of the tracks you were born, you have a choice as to how to respond to any given situation. Therefore, I chose not to permit anyone, or anything, to keep me from reaching my life's goals. The foundations and principles of our lives, and the cultivation of this country's visions, are the basis of the significant accomplishments within this nation.

Our success, as a nation, hinges on the decisions we make as voters throughout the course of our lives. Most of us in this country have made nearly all of our political and economic decisions based on our own cultural common knowledge approach to life. We have a hard time perceiving, or accepting, the points of view of others. This cultural common knowledge approach to governing is flawed. It has made it a difficult task for most Americans to share in this nation's power and wealth.

There are many pressing challenges facing this nation. We must utilize our Constitution's imperfections and transform them into productive economic values. This will allow us to create innovative economic tools that will

> "My dream is of a place and a time where America will once again be seen as the last best hope of earth."
>
> **Abraham Lincoln**

enhance the Constitution and the people it serves. These innovative tools will also lend a hand in restoring our nation's wealth.

We need a new economic mind-set in this country, a proactive approach to the ways our federal and state governments function economically. With a new economic focus, we can move our country forward, cost-effectively, without misappropriating the taxpayer's investment in their government. This innovative economic approach will reshape how commerce and wealth in this country are responsibly delivered.

We have an obligation, as a people, to gain knowledge from the errors of our past experiences. This knowledge will provide us with the meaningful steps with which to fix our nation's economic problems. That is why it is extremely vital that we learn from our past experiences, or we will be doomed, as a country, to repeat them.

As citizens, we must collectively come together and realize that the imperfections in our lives are the building blocks to one's success. Therefore, for anyone to become successful in life, regardless of one's life circumstances, one must proactively learn the skills needed to turn these imperfections into pathways for their success.

The assurance of being liberated from our nations past injustices have developed into an economic burden for us and our government. This hunger for truth and justice for all is the basic quality of God within humanity. It is fitting and constitutional that we search for the cause of our cultural and economic discontentment within our government, and each other. However, it is imperative for our nation to explore all levels of our society for an economic solution to this nation's past errors.

> *Do not dwell in the past, do not dream of the future, concentrate the mind on the present moment."*
>
> **Buddha**

The most difficult challenge that we face as a nation today is, how to move this country forward with regard to the discussion of the illusion of race and economic disparity. Presently, most politicians have chosen the path to self-indulgence, instead of standing firm on the course for individual freedom.

Americans have a responsibility to their families, as well as a duty to our country, to create the atmosphere of expectation, not just for themselves, but also for others. Today, we are suffering from the economic and social problems of the past. These problems will continue as long as American citizens persist on viewing our country's past imperfections as being natural and unsolvable.

The aftermath of slavery and the Civil War are not typical conditions to be put aside. They are certainly not natural and should be dealt with respectfully. These past offenses have caused many in this country to suffer economically. As a nation we can no longer overlook these divisive issues, or its victims. The process of moving this nation forward, proactively and respectfully, must out-weigh the imperfections of the past.

There are some Americans who continue to blame others for our past cultural and economic injustices, while others avoid and reject these same issues out of fear. These rejections of past cultural and economic injustices continue to influence our political decisions today. These issues are preventing our country, and its citizens, from moving economically forward.

Throughout this book, we have addressed the importance of acknowledging our past imperfections as not being natural to the human condition. Whenever possible, we must face our nations past imperfections directly and realistically. The physical sides of Slavery and the Civil War are over. However, both the economic and emotional side effects continue to wreak havoc on our society.

This book has demonstrated, without a doubt, that Americans of African descent are not the only ethnic group who are economically and emotionally suffering from the boomerang effects of Slavery and the Civil War's past. We have exposed the truth about the Three-Fifths Compromise agreement and how it has reversed the constitutional rule of law for almost everyone.

Some issues discussed throughout this book will be painful for some, but they must be discussed out of respect for this nation's dignity. The unproductive language of the Three-Fifths Compromise agreement is counterproductive to Americans way of life. It is an undemocratic process that is turning the middle class into the new form of slavery, and the poor into the new indentured servant.

We all know that certain forms of suffering are inevitable in any nation. Yet, the misery of slavery, the anguish caused by the Three-Fifths Compromise and the casualties of the Civil War, were all self- inflicted.

The universal level of economic satisfaction has improved life for many in America, because of today's technology. This satisfaction has allowed us not to be concerned over the anguish of others. It is this attitude that has prompted a fundamental constitutional shift in our assessment of past offenses. It makes it seem as if no one really cares. As a people, we do not want to comprehend the fundamental nature of our faults or perceive what is terribly amiss within our country.

The failure of our legal system is the continual presence of the Three-Fifths Compromise agreement within the Constitution. It is an infringement of our constitutional rights. This compromise provision presently poses a hidden danger to each and every one of us in this country.

The 'Why Me' Attitude

Most Americans of African descent, and the European descendents of the Civil War era, think of their own suffering as something that

> *If you want to make beautiful music, you must play the black and the white notes together.*
>
> **Richard M. Nixon**

has happened only to them and their ancestors. This mind-set of the 'why me' attitude, makes it not much of a leap to look for someone to hold accountable for their present day economic hardships.

As individuals, we sometimes fix our sights on the wrongs of the past and blame others. This 'why me' attitude allows individuals to continue being the victims of that past. This misgiving, or the feeling that you are being victimized because of your skin color, or your station in life, is all too familiar in this country.

One must remember that we live in a Republic/Democracy where it is each individual's responsibility to write their own economic future, with the assistance of their government. We cannot continue to blame others for the past if we do not do our part in bringing this nation forward economically.

We must stop pointing fingers and blaming others for the past, without having a means for correcting it. If we don't, we will continue to bring ourselves, and this nation, more psychological and economic suffering. Blaming others only brings the related feelings of anger, frustration and resentment upon us and to our federal government. We not only bring about our own complications with our gloomy thoughts of the past, but we also increase and amplify our past injustices in the same process.

We must remember that in this country there are countless victimizers at play, our dysfunctional government, our educational system and our failing families. However, most of the time, believe it or not, we the citizens victimize ourselves by how we vote. We continue to view ourselves as being the victims of the federal government.

It is essential for us to move past this wall of shame and to stop victimizing ourselves. We must begin to see ourselves as conquerors, and correct every constitutional imperfection that appears to hold us, and our nation, back. To do this, one must become a forward thinker, realizing that the past is just that, the past.

Who Are These Forward Thinkers ?

Forward thinkers are men and women who love and appreciate this nation. They love their country so much that they would lay down their life to defend it. Why would anyone contemplate dying for their country? Could it be that they have faith in the language within the Constitution? Or, do they feel some kind of loyalty to the Union? Could it be that their social environment transformed them into what we now call forward thinkers? The majority of forward thinkers believe that they can control their own density.

I believe these men and women, like myself, have learned through life experience how to conquer their fears of the past. Men and women who desire to become forward thinkers must understand that they have an innate ability to turn any form of imperfections or errors into proactive values.

We must recognize that we cannot alter the past, but we can correct it. Consciously, we know that no human being can reverse time to alter its outcome. The errors of the past should be thought of as a tool for correction.

> "Surely God would not have created such a being as man, with an ability to grasp the infinite, to exist only for a day! No, no, man was made for immortality."
>
> **Abraham Lincoln**

As a nation, we can turn our past imperfections or errors in judgment into direct and realistic expectations for change. The Three-Fifths Compromise agreement is this nation's biggest blunder, after slavery. And as a basic rule of thumb, there are no imperfections, or errors, within our Constitution that cannot be resolved. We are a nation of laws and we have the constitutional tools to right these errors of judgment. Imperfection in a wise man is the means by which he corrects himself. Our Constitution is designed the very same way.

Whatever your ethnicity or your cultural beliefs, we must cease to complain about the past and direct our nation's energies toward proactive changes. Within this nation we have many traditions that are part of

> "Conformity is the jailer of freedom and the enemy of growth."
>
> **John F. Kennedy**

our psychological hardships. These may seem natural to some. There are also times in this country that we are overly sensitive to insignificant things we cannot change.

This negative thinking process increases our personal pain and suffering. However, failure to correct these injustices of the past will only reinforce these negative afflictions, which make problems in this country seem so much worse. Regardless of what happens to us in our lives, good or bad, we can choose our reaction and find ways to lessen the pain. We can, and we must, refrain from reacting negatively and not let the cultural insults of others control our positive way of thinking.

In this way, we can protect ourselves from those feelings of hurt, and betrayal, that can become a natural state of mind when we are always thinking negatively. We cannot always escape negative complex situations, such as cultural animosities. We can choose our responses to these situations and at the same time minimize the extent of our suffering.

> "A pessimist is one who makes difficulties of his opportunities and an optimist is one who makes opportunities of his difficulties."
>
> **Harry S. Truman**

We must also realize that our country cannot heal itself without the constructive participation of its citizens in the healing process. Our psychological tendency in this country is to devalue what has occurred in the past and to limit our sight upon ourselves. This unconstructive pattern of thinking is a major source of misery within our country. It has a demoralizing impact on us all.

Most times, we imagine ourselves to be the center of the universe, and we become downhearted or infuriated when we realize that others do not think or feel the same. Problems will invariably arise in our daily lives that seem normal. Most problems in our country do not automatically create suffering for millions, as has the Three-Fifths Compromise agreement.

> "Change your thoughts and you change your world."
>
> **Norman Vincent Peale**

It is imperative that we, as a nation, deal directly with these constitutional imperfections that are affecting millions. We must address the Three-Fifths Compromise agreement directly, and then focus our energies into finding solutions to transform this flawed agreement into challenges that will benefit our nation.

Earlier in this chapter, we discussed the significance of experiencing suffering as an abnormal reality of human existence. By accepting this truth, we must find positive and productive ways to deal with the reality that one does suffer unfairly in this country because of the color of their skin. Many of our ancestors had to endure the economic, physical, sociological and psychological impacts of Slavery and the Civil War.

Therefore, as a nation, we must assist the descendants of both Slavery and those European descendants of the Civil War. We have an obligation and a constitutional duty to discover proactive ways to deal with the after-math of these internal shames.

The pain of both Slavery and the Civil War are interconnected. The people's faith in this living, timeless document is interconnected as well. For this nation to move forward, we should objectively analyze our true vision of justice. To change our Constitution's imperfections into proactive goals, it is imperative to examine the causes and origins of our resistance to change. We must also examine the misfortunes that are left behind because of our inactions.

> *"Once you say you're going to settle for second, that's what happens to you in life."*
>
> **John F. Kennedy**

For citizens to appreciate the process for change, they must understand that the nature of our existence, as a Union, depends on it. It is the nature of all things in life to evolve every moment. This should indicate to us that all things lack the ability to stay the same. All things in life, even our constitutional rule of law, must eventually evolve.

Our rule of law cannot exist in a permanent state. No crisis in our country, no matter how challenging or comfortable it is, can remain the same under its own self-determining power. Consequently, all things under the power, or influence, of the universe remain out of our control. Though, in the case of our constitutional rule of law, we can control its power and we can control how it presides over us.

So, at any given moment in our country, no matter how pleasant or agreeable your experience is at the time, things never stay the same. Our constitutional rule of law must evolve for our nation to survive for the next generation. To the degree that we refuse to accept this fact, and resist the natural order of change, some of us try desperately to cling to a flawed past. We do this because we know

> *Our lives begin to end the day we become silent about things that matter"*
>
> **Martin Luther King, Jr.**

that we cannot control the future. We persist in bringing about our own suffering by holding on to that past, in ignorance.

Holding on to the Three-Fifths Compromise agreement is not a noble act, but amending it is. Amending this compromise provision will not weaken our national security or economically bankrupt us. What it will do is bring our country nearer to that of one of perfection. We must look at our past problems from a different perspective other than just our own.

To fix our eyes on past events, from a different perspective, can be very beneficial to our nation's development. The ability to alter our perspective on life is the most powerful tool God has given mankind. To utilize the constitutional rule of law to assist us through life's every day dilemmas, is a powerful tool designed by man. We must realize that every incident and every event that happens in this nation can have a different outcome.

For example; in my own case, my ancestors lost their country, their heritage and their traditions to slavery. Technically and constitutionally, because of this Three-Fifths Compromise agreement, the descendents of African slaves in this country are still legally deemed as refugees within their own nation.

> *If a society cannot help the many who are poor, it cannot save the few who are rich.*
>
> **John F. Kennedy**

The language of this Compromise stated that the total number of dark ethnic groups was legally deemed to be three-fifths of its total. This means that three-fifths of this population was not constitutionally equal to the whole of the privileged population. This reversal of civil

> *You cannot escape the responsibility of tomorrow by evading it today.*
>
> **Abraham Lincoln**

liberties of the Non-Caucasian population has led to the economic and social predicament that we, as a nation, face today.

Slavery was one of the tragic and horrific events that happened to the ancestors of African Americans. The Civil War was also one of the most tragic and horrific of events to happened to both the ancestors, and the descendents, of Caucasian Americans and African Americans.

As an American of African descent who is experiencing the aftermath of slavery's past, and the economic pains of the Three-Fifths Compromise agreement, I began to realize something. I have the innate ability to proactively alter my perspective on Slavery itself. This new perspective gave me the literary confidence needed to compose this manuscript.

Therefore, from my viewpoint, my African American ancestors and the ancestors of Caucasian Americans, both having fought in the Civil War, did not die in vain. They died for a constitutional process, and within that flawed process, freedom was formed. Not just my freedom, but freedom for all of us who breathe on American soil.

The reality is, Slavery, the Three-Fifths compromise agreement and the Civil War, almost destroyed this nation's anticipation for perfection. As a nation, we will not be able to get past the pains and anguish of Slavery and the Civil War, until we learn to respect and make amends for that flawed past.

> "Nothing in all the world is more dangerous than sincere ignorance and conscientious stupidity."
>
> **Martin Luther King, Jr.**

Every American regardless of their ethnicity, is paying a high price for the divisiveness of our politicians. We live in difficult times and we continue to deny our past. This denial of the past will insure that we will repeat it in the future. Let us not complain or even debate the past without a means of correcting

> *"When even one American- who has done nothing wrong - is forced by fear to shut his mind and close his mouth - then all Americans are in peril."*
>
> **Harry S. Truman**

it. The past for me is, just that, the past.

The dreadful economic and emotional effects of Slavery and the Civil War experience must be treated as an error in man's judgment. For only God can judge the moral acts of Slavery and the Civil War. However, if the Three-Fifths Compromise is not amended soon, its negative effects will continue to play an unpleasant part in our nation's economic future. Knowing that we can change and resolve this constitutional flaw is essential for this nation to move forward in its economic development.

The problem with debating how to resolve Slavery's past and the Three-Fifths Compromise, without our nation truly appreciating the Civil War experience, has made this debate a one sided issue. Both political parties seem to have forgotten the impoverished Caucasian victim, and the economic and psychological pain the Civil War experience caused them and their descendants.

Americans of African descent, along with their Caucasian brothers and sisters, have both been victims to these acts of Slavery and the Civil War. It is these imperfections, the Civil War and Slavery's past, that has allowed us to become a Multi-ethnic nation, as well as, a prosperous country.

As a nation, we should not make the mistake of attempting to make the descendents of slavery's past economically whole, without making the impoverished European descendents of the Civil War economically whole, as well. America cannot constitutionally, economically or culturally move forward without including both the victims of Slavery and the victims of the Civil War at the same time.

We must look at the unfortunate experience of Slavery, the Three-Fifths Compromise and the Civil War, with the expectation of changing these imperfections into practical tools that will help this nation to become the source of hopefulness. What is that hopefulness? That hopefulness is contained within the living and timeless words of our Constitution.

Our Constitution as a whole has some imperfections, but that is okay. That is why the Founders purposely designed the language of Constitution to allow for change. They knew that change would be the only way for this nation to reach its goals of expectations.

As a descendent of slaves I learned, from my parents, that the only way I could free myself from slavery's past was to learn to forgive my country for creating that past. It is my present day perspective of the past that allows me to free myself, and others, from the emotional after effects of Slavery and the Civil War.

The grief of being subjected to the aftermath of slavery, as well as being blessed with the tools of forgiveness, has greatly benefited me. It has allowed me to move forward in my quest for economic-wellness. I discovered, through the noble parts of the Constitution, that the key to a successful life in this country is to seize the past, and learn from it, and then take the time to correct it. That is what our Founding Fathers struggled to do in our Constitution.

Often it seems that when a problem arises in our country that is unpleasant, such as debates over cultural animosity, we don't want to confront them proactively. As we compare our past mistakes with other nations who have had similar unpleasant incidents, it will help us to look at our imperfections from a different perspective. We must view our nation's imperfections as tools for improving the Constitution. Once we begin to view our problems from a proactive point of view, they will appear less significant and less overwhelming.

There have been many honorable and rewarding experiences in our nation's past. We have overcome many tests and trials, and we can certainly learn from our past as we redesign our visions for the future. We have had some great leaders in the past whose life's goal was to keep this union together, at any cost. Some lost their life for it.

This was re-echoed in a similar warning made by James Madison, the architect of the Three-Fifths Compromise agreement. He said, "It's the people who are the guardians of this Constitution, they are the oath keepers. Their eyes must be ever ready to mark, their voice to pronounce, and their arms to repel or repair, aggressions on the authority of the laws of the Constitution."

The fraudulent language within this compromise provision has placed America in a state of disunion. This disunion is our failure, as citizens, to accept the fact; that the Three-Fifths Compromise agreement is the enemy of the states. Not until we accept the fact, that this compromise provision is our true enemy, can we fashion a constitutional solution.

After ten years of research and the writing of this manuscript I came to the awareness, that no matter what we say, or do, to facilitate this nation's greatness, only we, as citizens, can fix it. I have put my heart and soul into these words in the hope that they will strengthen our country.

All of our visions and ideas come to life once we understand our role and our financial responsibilities to this nation. My desire is that the words within this book will bring men and women from income despair to economic success. The keys to your economic success' are embedded within our constitutional rule of law.

Within this book we have revealed why the Three-Fifths Compromise is the enemy to our economic wellness. We have also revealed how some politicians, and the status quo, continue to utilize the flawed Three-Fifths Compromise agreement for political positioning. There has been a deep cultural resentment in this country, born out of our laziness and dislike of others, because of this compromise provision.

We fail to understand, as citizens, what is expected of us. Often our normal tendency is to try to blame our problems on the past, and on others. However, we are called upon, as citizens, not only to be right in our hearts, but also to be right in our thinking. You and I, my friend, are entitled from this nation only the freedom of choice, and even that you have to earn.

It is your faith and trust in this Constitution that will give you a new perspective on your responsibility to the Union. Even President Lincoln understood that line of reasoning. The secret to his success as president was that he purposely surrendered his intelligence to the Constitution. The Constitution was his legal guide. He understood that the nature of our nation's existence depended on its evolving and governing power. .

He also had a vision of a *pro-ethnic society,* where multi-ethnicity would be the American heritage. Whenever problems pressed on him, Lincoln had, within himself, the divine remembrance that every problem that a citizen would face in this nation could be solved by using the noble language of the Constitution. President Lincoln understood that this Constitution was the doorway to men's free-will and their desires.

One of Lincoln famous quotes of August 22, 1862, was in a Letter to Horace Greeley stating, "My paramount objective in this struggle is to save the Union, and is not either to save or to destroy slavery. If I could save the Union without freeing any slave I would do it, and if I could save it by freeing all the slaves I would do it; and if I could save it by freeing some and leaving

> *My great concern is not whether you have failed, but whether you are content with your failure."*
>
> **Abraham Lincoln**

others alone I would also do that. What I do about Slavery and the colored race, I do because I believe it helps to save the Union and what I forbear, I forbear because I do not believe it would help to save the Union. I shall do less whenever I shall believe what I am doing hurts the cause, and I shall do more whenever I shall believe doing more will help the cause." This letter to Horace Greeley demonstrated the depth of Lincoln's commitment to the Constitution and not to the elites of this nation. The noble language within this Constitution was President Lincoln's *source of hope as well as his honor*. He lived and he died by these words, freeing a Union from the nightmare of Slavery and the Civil War.

President Lincoln understood that the unperfected languages of this Constitution could be used as tools to move this nation forward to its perfection. What will you do for the Union? Where do you stand on these problems? The choice is yours.

Every single problem faced by our nation today was set in motion by human behavior. Since our behavior is the root cause of our problems, we have the power, insight and constitutional tools to change our imperfections into accomplishments.

Citizens who can appreciate the methods of forward thinking, understand how to utilize our constitutional errors as tools for correcting past injustices. These same citizens should also understand that it is their constitutional responsibility to also protect economically, those who came before them.

9

CHALLENGES
FOR A NATION

To have a productive debate, or deal with any challenges we face as a nation, we need to establish a central focal point on which all parties can agree. If we can agree on the fact that every economic problem we face as a nation was set in motion by human behavior, we should be able to agree on a constitutional remedy. We have the constitutional tools, as well as the insight, to resolve our disagreements in a proactive way.

Throughout this book you have heard us mention many times that the Three-Fifths Compromise agreement, and the language it contains, is unconstitutional and unproductive. This book, "Wolves and Their Prey", is not like other books, which only complain about our nation's problems and never give realistic solutions. We have made it our mission to make available, within this chapter, constitutional fixes for each and every problem that has been presented.

Therefore, to begin the process of moving this country economically and culturally forward, we need to re-establish the fundamental act of True Conservatism. It is this act of True Conservatism that allowed man to fight for this nation's independence. It was this act of True Conservatism that gave man the courage, and the moral conviction, to abolished slavery. It is this act of True Conservatism that integrated a nation. And, from these struggles, the United States of America was formed.

The challenge for us today is, how do we develop respect for one another's cultural point of view? Respecting other's points of view is the building block for a successful nation. Knowing our nation has many challenges, we must begin these debates on issues in which we can all agree.

Can we agree that the constitutional rule of law that governs our lives is sound? Can we also agree that, regardless of our ethnicity, every American has, and is, benefiting from the noble parts of the Constitution? Most importantly, can we agree that some of our lawmakers are purposefully leading this nation down the wrong economic path for their own political gain?

Before beginning to write this book, I debated within myself as to whether my views on the Three-Fifths Compromise agreement were unfounded. However, after one has examined this book, and agrees with the assessment that this compromise agreement is unconstitutional, what will you do to help solve this crisis?

There are many challenges, as a nation, which we can either ignore or correct. We cannot continue to ignore the economic and psychological hardship of this compromise provision on the American people. Our most pressing challenge presently is, how do we utilize these constitutional errors in judgment and transform them into productive economic values.

> "We can't solve problems by using the same kind of thinking we used when we created them."
>
> **Albert Einstein**

Correcting these constitutional errors will allow us to create innovative financial and legal tools that will enhance the Constitution, the States, and the people it serves. These innovative tools will also assist us in restoring our nation's wealth, as well as its honor. How do we accomplish these objectives, when we have been listening for years to career politicians, with their never-ending TV sound bites? Some political leaders are using fraudulent language to confuse and dampen the spirit of Americans. Due to this deceptive language, most citizens feel a sense of disconnectedness toward their government, and their political leaders.

These career politicians want us to view our national debt and cultural problems as being too large, complex, and beyond our comprehension. Yet, we are paying a high price for our anti-government views and our willingness to run away from

> *"The vote is the most powerful instrument ever devised by man for breaking down injustice and destroying the terrible walls which imprison men because they are different from other men.."*

> *We the people are the rightful masters of both Congress and the courts, not to overthrow the Constitution but to overthrow the men who pervert the Constitution.*
>
> **Abraham Lincoln**

our problems. People who are anti-government, or those who believe in rapid changes to our legal systems, are in total opposition to our individual liberties and the fundamentals of True Conservatism.

As a people, we have become lazy and have forfeited our economic and legal control by handing it to the politicians. These same politicians continually refuse to face major economic challenges that would be a benefit to the average American. Because of our laziness, we have become blinded to the facts before us. Our children and grandchildren will pay a high price for our acts of defiance and resistance to change.

We challenge you, the reader, with a call to action, to learn the truth about your economic and constitutional privileges as a citizen. But with these economic privileges also come financial rewards. Learning to create wealth, and saving that wealth, is one of our many economic responsibilities.

The reader must focus on his or her understanding of their economic rights as guaranteed by the Constitution. It is our responsibility, and not that of Congress, to know when our civil liberties have been violated. However, it is our constitutional duty to know how to protect ourselves, and our families, from the economic mistakes being perpetrated in Congress.

> "Any change is resisted because bureaucrats have a vested interest in the chaos in which they exist."
>
> **Richard M. Nixon**

Citizens Petition

Every American at birth receives a constitutional privilege. This privilege is the gift of Citizens Petition. We have been granted a constitutional provision that allows individuals to petition their State or Federal Government for legal or economic redress. The authority of Citizens Petition allows Americans to address Congress directly, without the assistance of politicians or lobbyists. The Citizens Petition gives every citizen the constitutional tool that separates them from special interest groups.

The right to petition your State or Federal Government insures that the scales of economic justice are always balanced. Few Americans know of their constitutional right when it comes to petitioning. Those that know about Citizens Petition do not know how to utilize its authority effectively. We cannot wait for Wall-Street, Main Street or our Government to make economic changes for us. Citizens have no other practical legal or constitutional alternatives for economic changes, except through the use of the Citizens Petitions.

A Cultural Mind-Set

The older generations, those sixty-five years of age or older, were raised during the wealthiest and the most cultural intolerant period in American history. Our government was more efficient in the use of their tax dollars and in the deliverance of many of the basic promises.

These promises include getting a decent education and the raising of individual living standards, as well as personal security. Therefore, when it comes to the expenditure of our nation's resources, the older generation has little or no incentive to make the slightest of fundamental changes in Washington's economic policies.

Some seniors have become accustomed to their post World War II prosperity and are spellbound by their period of history. Some are also caught up in today's political distortion. They tend to judge new economic ideas by their deep-seated values and fears.

Their actions are understandable; since no citizen wants to give up any assets they have earned, or lose any constitutional benefits granted to them. And for those citizens who are looking for economic change, they must understand that with economic change comes the responsibility to protect our seniors, who are our nation's most vital assets.

FOUR CHALLENGES THAT WILL FACILITATE OUR ECONOMIC GROW

CHALLENGE#1
Amending Two Constitutional Errors
1. **Article One, Section Two, Paragraph Three**
The Three-Fifths Compromise agreement
2. **Article One, Section Nine, Paragraph One**
The Powers Prohibited to Congress.

CHALLENGE#2
The Correction of Two Governmental Crimes
1. District of Columbia Emancipation Act
2. The confiscation of private lands.

CHALLENGE#3
Reversing the Effects of Reverse Discrimination

CHALLENGE#4
Revamping Our Immigration and Naturalization Policies

CHALLENGE #1:

<u>Amending Two Constitutional Errors</u>

The first Constitutional error that must be amended is the Three-Fifths Compromise agreement. This fraudulent language resides within Article One, Section Two, Paragraph Three of the Constitution. This compromise provision is a cultural and economic strain on every American. It makes it a political struggle for politicians to fashion proactive laws that will economically benefit all Americans.

The second of these constitutional errors is Article One, Section Nine, Paragraph one, "The Powers Prohibited to Congress". From 1787 to 1808, this article denied Congress the power to restrain the flow of migration and the importation of slaves into the United States. A federal import tax of ten dollars was also placed on each slave imported by the Southern states. The profits from this Federal Government taxation program were approximately one hundred-sixty million dollars in tax revenue. "The Powers Prohibited to Congress", is a constitutional deception, designed by the status quo of the time, to take advantage of the Commerce Clause.

THE SOLUTION:

Knowing our past history, how do we as citizens begin the task of correcting these two constitutional defects? The only realistic solution is to proactively utilize the First Amendment. This amendment was designed to give the individual citizen the privilege to petition their Federal Government for redress.

The petitions that most people sign in front of grocery stores only require you to be a registered voter. This type of everyday petition is an outpouring of public support for a position or belief held by certain organizations. While a Citizens Petition is the actual first step of an individual's legal challenge to a government policy. As citizens, we must confront these constitutional defects with the pen of petitioning.

Only when millions of Americans begin to individually petition Congress, can these constitutional errors be eliminated. Knowing how to petition effectively is just as important as voting. It is the only constitutional tool that citizens have with which to fight back against lawmakers who continue to use the illusion of race to exploit the will of the people.

If you feel that we are incorrect in our assessment of these constitutional defects, or that the Three-Fifths Compromise does not personally affect you economically, we respect your opinion. Should you feel that we are right, and you fail to voice your opposition to this compromise provision, our country will continue to reap the economic and psychological hardships caused by this compromise agreement and our inaction.

Our goal is to have, within five years, the majority of Americans take part in a nationwide Citizens Petition drive to change how commerce functions. Congress and the Courts are constitutionally obligated to process all petitions and to take full responsibility for the unsound legislation of past legislators.

It is also the responsibility of every citizen to cast their votes and to use his or her power of petition to compel Congress to resolve all past legislative errors. These Citizens Petitions will insure that those who are elected, appointed or hired to the Federal Government, will comply with the demands of their constituents, as well as earn their salaries.

> *One person with a belief is equal to a force of ninety-nine who have only interests.*
>
> **Peter Marshall**

Citizens Petition would also guarantee that every citizen, regardless of their ethnicity, would not have to bear any of the economic burdens created by past legislators. The Federal Government has many financial resources with which to pay the victims of these constitutional errors, without the use of our tax dollars.

CHALLENGE # 2

<u>*Correcting Two Governmental Crimes*</u>

The first of these governmental crimes was the "District of Columbia Emancipation Act", signed into law April 16, 1862, by President Abraham Lincoln. This particular Emancipation Act was to insure that Washington D. C. slave owners would be compensated

> "If a free society cannot help the many who are poor, it cannot save the few who are rich."
>
> **John F. Kennedy**

a maximum of three hundred dollars for each of their human properties surrendered to the Federal Government.

For political reasons, the Federal Government dispensed more than a million dollars in tax revenues to purchase approximately 3,100 slaves. This act was in anticipation of President Abraham Lincoln's decision to abolished slavery. The District of Columbia Emancipation Act was a legal method in which the congressional leaders could estimate the cost to deport all African refugees from American soil. The District of Columbia Emancipation Act also allowed bureaucrats in office to turn a profit by denying basic human rights.

The second of these governmental crimes was the unconstitutional confiscation of the two million acres of land that was given to the African refugee's for their military service during the Civil War. President Andrew Johnson, a Southern Democrat, had these lands confiscated from the African refugees.

This allocation of two million acres of land was President Abraham Lincoln's, and the Republican Party's, first attempt to establish reparation, or compensation, to African refugees for their military service. This attempt at reparation was not a down payment for the enslavement endured by the African people. Though it was a form of restitution, which would have allowed African refugees an economic chance to assimilate into the American way of life.

THE SOLUTION:

The solutions to these particular problems are twofold. First, a federal lawsuit must be enacted to demand that the federal government return the million dollars in tax revenues for the District of Columbia Emancipation Act. And secondly, petition Congress to return the profits from these confiscated lands.

It is essential that these profits be utilized to educate the underprivileged in the proper use of credit and money management. These programs must be proactive in their methods, which will assist the victims to acquire a higher education, affordable homes, or start businesses. This will help millions of citizen's break free from the grip of welfare, and thereby creating billions in tax revenues.

CHALLENCE #3

Reversing the Effects of Reverse Discrimination

Our third challenge is to uncover methods that will limit the boomerang effects of reverse discrimination. Historically, cultural/reverse discrimination was primarily directed toward persons whose skin color, or cultural beliefs, were different from those of the status quo. For the first time in our nation's history, reverse discrimination is now affecting all Americans, regardless of one's ethnicity.

THE SOLUTION:

The solution is simple. We must revamp our Affirmative Action programs for the Twenty-First century. Though, there are some politicians who desire the elimination of Affirmative Action programs all together. Removing, or eliminating, affirmative action would only exacerbate the cultural struggle over one ethnic group dominating the workplace. Affirmative Action policies are designed to protect a person's race, disability, gender, ethnic origin, and age. Regardless of what some politicians claim, there are no policies within the affirmative action programs excluding Caucasian Americans from its protection.

CHALLENGE#4

Overhaul Our Immigration and Naturalization Policies

Our fourth and final challenge is to overhaul our Immigration and Naturalization Policies. Our immigration and naturalization laws are both incoherent and unconstitutional, because they are based on cultural profiling. The Three-Fifths compromise agreement has rendered the immigration policies moot to the majority of American people. These policies do not allow for the normal process of assimilation to a large segment of our population.

The Solution:

We must begin the process of bringing our immigration policies into the Twenty-First century. As citizens, we should compel our lawmakers to do their constitutional duties. Included in their duties is having respect for this nation's growing diversity. Our nation's Immigration and Naturalization policies must reflect the needs of all of its citizens and not just those of the status quo.

These solutions must also include revamping the Commerce Clause to constitutionally represent all segments of the population. It will be up to the newly formed Citizens Coalitions to help come up with realistic answers to the growing feelings of disconnectedness and animosity within our diverse society. These citizens coalitions will be operating in every precinct of every state. It is essential that we develop innovative and inclusive immigration policies. Finally, these new immigration policies should be profitable for the citizen, the States and our Federal Government.

Throughout our nation's development each generation has had to make sacrifices. Now is the time for the present generation to make their sacrifice and take their place in this nation's history. American's must accept the fact that the government has not failed them, but it is they who have failed their government.

> *"You have to learn the rules of the game. And then you have to play better than anyone else."*
>
> **Albert Einstein**

Americans do not appreciate the diversity of this nation, nor do they want the responsibility of being the guardians of the country's wealth. We blindly delegate our constitutional responsibilities to politicians who continue to promote the status quo.

When compared to many of the world's population, we should be grateful for our economic and personal freedoms. Many Americans are justifiably angry over the problems that have been dumped upon us by past and present Congress'. But voting in anger and pointing fingers at politicians, while failing to do our part as citizens, is both lazy and insincere.

Yesterday's Solutions

Americans must come to the understanding that our leaders in Congress are trying to resolve our nation's problems with yesterday's solutions. The solutions that worked for the status quo in the past will not work for us today. Americans, young and old, must work together to insure that our constitutional rule of law functions correctly for all.

It is the responsibility of every citizen to participate in the healing of our nation's economic and cultural impasses. The process of healing can only materialize if we compel our political leaders to implement future proactive solutions. The politics of subjection and rejection should be the obsessions of the past

New solutions are what are needed to encourage new attitudes. These new attitudes will lead us away from the mindset of blindly following our political leaders. That is why it is imperative to form citizens coalitions within each state. These citizens coalitions will focus on innovative methods by which to motivate millions to petition for economic change.

These petitioning coalitions will insure that our political leaders comply fully with their constitutional responsibility. Their responsibilities are to represent all of their constituents, regardless of their ethnicity or position in life.

The Framers believed the right of petition to be a fundamental freedom. This constitutional entitlement is given to each American at birth, as well as to those who are naturalized. The right to petition has never been utilized by individual citizens on a large scale. Therefore, we must make a greater effort to utilize these tools in a proactive way to revolutionize our economic future.

The foundation of our Constitution, and its amendments, are behind the times and new amendments are needed. But when those amendments are added, they must be in line with the methodology of True Conservatism. America is in a semi-permanent state of economic uncertainty and unrest, because new solutions brought to the table are being rejected by the status quo.

The policymakers of the twenty-first century are constitutionally required to bring forth bold new constitutional provisions that will benefit all Americans. This would enable

Washington to move our nation forward economically with specific incremental steps.

Petitioning Our Government

We need to work toward making citizen's petitioning a major part of our political agenda. This means that millions of individuals, regardless of their financial status, will petition Congress to make these economic changes a reality. This book has outlined many constitutional imperfections, but these errors will not be resolved during one session of Congress or, for that matter, in one Presidency.

The foundations of our Union, and that of our American way of life, are dependent on the success of these corrections. Americans have both a moral and a constitutional obligation to right these wrongs. The noble articles of our constitutional rule of law, when used correctly, will permit us to amend the Three-Fifths Compromise agreement with humility.

A Call for Action

We simply cannot undo the decades of reckless leadership. But we can prevent it from further destroying our country and our future. Since the establishment of our country there have been many historical accomplishments. The list begins with our separation from Great Britain, abolishing the physical side of slavery, and promoting the suffrage of women. These accomplishments also include the safety net during the Great Depression, the defeat of Nazi Germany during World War II and the winning of modest civil rights for millions in the 1960's.

It is time for Americans to lay aside the skepticisms of their government and take a stand for our economic futures. That is why, we can either vote for noble reasons or for our own self preservation. But in either case, we must vote and petition our government for economic change.

Throughout this text, we have focused on three major challenges. The first was to present to the people the constitutional tools necessary for their economic success. Secondly, we demonstrated that there are constitutional laws purposely designed to hinder the economic process of the majority of the American people. Third, we focused on teaching and promoting the fundamental theories of True Conservatism, upon which our Republican Democracy was built.

Moving forward with new economic agendas will insure that Americans will gain control over their economic future. Included are suggestions for personal and collective actions that will make a difference in the lives of many. Realistic and concrete solutions have been presented to some of the most difficult challenges facing our country today. But this is only the beginning.

Let's say, you are standing in the middle of the mall, and there is a 245 pound man with a gun running toward you. You can close your eyes or look the other way, and hope that he does not see you. Or you can do something, anything, to get out of his way.

America cannot continue to look the other way, or get out of the way, from the devastating effects of the flawed Three-Fifths Compromise. Nor can we continue to hide behind the fact that this defective compromise provision is the major cause of our economic and cultural problems. This compromise provision will continue to affect us until we collectively petition our Congress to resolve it

Meaningful steps are needed to resolve the issues of Slavery's past and the Civil War's tragedy, which continues to affect our national debt. These steps will be difficult, but by recognizing and resolving these underlying problems, our country will become a morally and economically healthier nation. Our nation will go 'nowhere' until we repair the economic, emotional and cultural divisions that are tearing our nation apart.

The negative impact of our failure to deal with our constitutional imperfections is immeasurable. These constitutional imperfections are slowly reversing our civil liberties. Let us reiterate, the governing charter of our lives is the noble and evolving language of the Constitution. Our country has come from 'nowhere' to where we are today, a prosperous and almost perfect union.

SOURCES AND
SUGGESTED READING

CHAPTER 2

What's right about the Theories of True Conservatism?

Political logic: defeating Conservative Theories of rationality.

Fred Sauer A Simple Guide: How Liberalism, A Euphemism for Socialism, Destroys Peoples and Nations.

What Is Conservatism and What Is Wrong with It? Agre, Philip E. (1995): My Top 10 Email Hassles.

Agre, Philip E. (1994): Surveillance and Capture: Two Models of Privacy.

Moore Stephen, "Government: America's 31 Growth industries." Institute for policy innovation, February 1993.

Peterson, Peter G. Facing up: How We Can save America for Our Children. New York: Hyperion 1993

The Three-Fifths Compromise, a Short Political Biography of Henry Clay

Bicameral Legislature the American Bicameral LegislatureBanning, Lance. *The Sacred Fire of Liberty: James Madison and the Founding of the Federal Republic* Ithaca, N.Y.: Cornell University Press, 1995.

Brant, Irving. *James Madison*. Indianapolis: Bobbs Merrill, 1941-61.

Channing, Edward. *The Jeffersonian System: 1801-1811*. New York: Greenwood Press, 1969.

Cooke, Jacob E., Ed. *The Federalist* Middletown, Conn.: Wesleyan University Press, 1982.

Elkins, Stanley M. and Eric L. McKitrick. *The Age of Federalism*. New York: Oxford University Press, 1993.

Hunt, Gaillard, Ed. *The Writings of James Madison*. New York: G. P. Putnam's Sons, 1900-10.

Hutchinson, William T., et al., Eds. *9*, 1962-1991.

Black, Jeremy. *War for America: The Fight for Independence, 1775–1783*. 2001. Analysis from a noted British military historian.

Benn, Carl. *Historic Fort York, 1793–1993*. Toronto: Dundurn Press Ltd., 1993.

Boatner, Mark Mayo, III. *Encyclopedia of the American Revolution*. 1966; revised 1974. Military topics, references many secondary sources.

Chambers, John Whiteclay II, ed. in chief. *The Oxford Companion to American Military History*. Oxford University Press, 1999.

Crocker III, H. W. (2006). *Don't Tread on Me*. New York: Crown Forum.

CHAPTER 3

Boston, Rob. 2000. *Close Encounters with the Religious Right: Journeys into the Twilight Zone of Religion and Politics*. Prometheus Books.

Boyd, James H., *Politics and the Christian Voter*

Bruns, Roger A. 2002. *Preacher: Billy Sunday and Big-Time American Evangelism*. University of Illinois Press.

Diamond, Sara. 1995. *Roads to Dominion: Right-Wing Movements and Political Power in the United States*. New York: Guilford. An attack from the left

Green, John C., James L. Guth and Kevin Hill. 1993. "Faith and Election: The Christian right in Congressional Campaigns 1978–1988." *The Journal of Politics* 55(1), (February): 80–91.

Green, John C. "The Christian Right and the 1994 Elections: A View from the States," *PS: Political Science and Politics* Vol. 28, No. 1 (Mar., 1995),

Himmelstein, Jerome L. 1990. *To The Right: The Transformation of American Conservatism*. University of California Press.

Marsden, George. *Understanding Fundamentalism and Evangelicalism.*

Martin, William. 1996. *with God on Our Side: The Rise of the Religious Right in America*, New York: Broadway Books.

Gottfried, Paul. *The Conservative Movement* Twayne, 1993.

Guttman, Allan. *The Conservative Tradition in America* Oxford University Press, 1967.

Americans with Disabilities Act of 1990, accessboard.gov

Summary of LGBT civil rights protections, by state, at Lambda Legal, lambdalegal.org

A useful survey is Paul Sieghart, The Lawful Rights of Mankind: An Introduction to the International Legal Code of Human Rights, Oxford University Press, 1985.

Mears, T. Lambert, Analysis of M. Ortolan's Institutes of Justinian, Including the History and, p. 75.

Fahlbusch, Erwin and Geoffrey William Bromiley, The encyclopedia of Christianity, Volume 4, p. 703.

CHAPTER 4

Hymowitz; Weissman (1975). A History of Women in America. Bantam.Schultz, Jeffrey D. (2002). Encyclopedia of Minorities in American Politics: African Americans and Asian Americans. p. 284.

Daniels, Roger. Coming to America, a History in Immigration and Ethnicity in American Life.

Growth, Accumulation, and Unproductive Activity: An Analysis of the Post-War U.S. Economy, Cambridge University Press, 1987.

Productivity and American Leadership: The Long View (with William Baume and Sue Anne Bate Blackman), M.I.T. Press, 1989; paperback, 1991. [Honorable Mention, Annual Awards for Excellence in Publishing.

The Information Economy: The Implications of Unbalanced Growth (with Lars Oberg and William Baume), the Institute for Research on Public Policy, 1989.

Competitiveness, Convergence, and International Specialization (with David Dollar), M.I.T. Press, 1993.

Alford, Mimi Beardsley & Newman, Judith. Once Upon A Secret (2010)

Ballard, Robert. Collision with History: The Search for John F. Kennedy's PT 109 (2002)

Barnes, John. John F. Kennedy on Leadership (2007)

Bihar, Joy Ann. The Allegany Seneca's and Kansu Dam: forced relocation through two generations (1998)

Blight, James G. "The Fog of War: Eleven Lessons from the Life of Robert S. McNamara" (2005)

Breuer, Carl. John F. Kennedy and the Second Reconstruction (1977)

Bugloss, Vincent. "Reclaiming History: The Assassination of President John F. Kennedy" (2007)

Burner, David. John F. Kennedy and a New Generation (1988)

Casey, Shaun. The Making of a Catholic President: Kennedy vs. Nixon 1960 (2009)

Collier, Peter & Horowitz, David. The Kennedys (1984)

Cottrell, John. Assassination! The World Stood Still (1964)

CHAPTER 5

Outline of a Theory of Practice (Cambridge Studies in Social and Cultural Anthropology). Cambridge University Press. Cohen,

A.P. 1985. *The Symbolic Construction of Community*. New York: Routledge.

Dawkins, Richard. 1976. *The Selfish Gene*.

Geertz, C. 2000. *The Interpretation of Cultures: Selected Essays*. Basic Books.

Hoult, T.F. 1969. *Dictionary of Modern Sociology*. Totowa, NJ: Littlefield, Adams & Co.

Professor Gregory Jay

Do Americans Share a Common Culture?

Birnbaum, Jonathan and Taylor, Clarence, eds. (2000). *Civil Rights since 1787: A Reader on the Black Struggle*, New York University Press Foner, Eric. *Reconstruction: America's Unfinished Revolution 1863–1877* (Harpercollins: 1988

Horton, James Oliver and Horton, Lois E. (1998). *In Hope of Liberty: Culture, Community and Protest among Northern Free Blacks, 1700–1860*

Litwack, Leon F. (1998). *Trouble in Mind: Black Southerners in the Age of Jim Crow*, Alfred A. Knopf

Litwack, Leon F (1980). *Been in the Storm So Long: The Aftermath of Slavery* Pulitzer Prize

John C. Frémont: the 1864 U.S. presidential candidate of the Radical Republicans.

John Bingham: U.S. Representative from Ohio and principal framer of the Fourteenth Amendment to the United States Constitution.

William Gannaway Brownlow: publisher of the *Knoxville Whig*; Tennessee Governor; U.S. Senator

Benjamin Butler: Massachusetts politician-soldier; hated by rebels for restoring control in New Orleans.

Zachariah Chandler: U.S. Senator from Michigan and Secretary of the Interior under Ulysses S. Grant.

Salmon P. Chase: U.S. Treasury Secretary under President Lincoln; Supreme Court chief justice; sought 1868 Democratic nomination as moderate.

James H. Lane: U.S. Senator from Kansas, leader of the Jayhawkers abolitionist movement.

Thaddeus Stevens: Radical leader in the U.S. House of Representatives from Pennsylvania.

Charles Sumner: U.S. Senator from Massachusetts; dominant Radical leader in Senate; specialist in foreign affairs; broke with Grant in 1872

Benjamin Wade: U.S. Senator from Ohio; he was next in line to become President if Johnson was removed

Henry Wilson: Massachusetts leader; Vice President under Grant

Ulysses S. Grant: President of the United States, signed Enforcement Acts and Civil Rights Act of 1875; General of the Army of the United States, supported Radical Reconstruction and Lowery, Charles D. and Marszalek, John F. (1992). *Encyclopedia of African-American Civil Rights: From Emancipation to the Present* Greenwood Press

Belz, Herman. *Abraham Lincoln, Constitutionalism and Equal Rights in the Civil War Era* Fordham University Press, 1998

Belz, Herman. *Emancipation and Equal Rights: Politics and Constitutionalism in the Civil War Era* (1978Belz, Herman. *A New Birth of Freedom: The Republican Party and Freedman's Rights, 1861-1866* (2000)

Benedict, Michael Les. *The Impeachment and Trial of Andrew Johnson* (1999)

Blackburn, George M. "Radical Republican Motivation: A Case History," *The Journal of Negro History,* Vol. 54, Castel, Albert E. *The Presidency of Andrew Johnson* (1979)

"Death List of a Day", p. 7, *New York Times*, 1899-3-26, Historical New York Times retrieved 2006-8-6 via

Thomas Clement Fletcher." *Dictionary of American Biography Base Set.* American Council of Learned Societies, 1928-1936. Reproduced in History Resource Center. Farmington Hills, MI: Gale Group.

CHAPTER 6

Appelbaum, Richard P. & Chambliss, William J. (1997). *Sociology: A Brief Introduction*. New York: Longman.

Barnett, Cynthia. (Undated). *The Measurement of White-Collar Crime Using Uniform Crime Reporting (UCR) Data*.

Clarke, Ronald (Ed). (1997). *Situational Crime Prevention: Successful Case Studies* (2nd edition). New York: Criminal Justice Press.

Dillon, Eamon Dilloninvestigates.com, *the Fraudsters – How Con Artists Steal Your Money Chapter 5, Pillars of Society, published September 2008 by Merlin Publishing, Ireland*

Friedrichs, David O. (2003) *Trusted Criminals: White Collar Crime in Contemporary Society*, Wadsworth. Geis, G., Meier, R. & Salinger, L. (eds.) (1995). *White-collar Crime: Classic & Contemporary Views*. NY: Free Press.

Green, Stuart P. (2006). *Lying, Cheating, and Stealing: A Moral Theory of White Collar Crime*. Oxford: Oxford University Press.

Sutherland, Edwin H. (1924) *Principles of Criminology*, Chicago: University of Chicago Press.

Sutherland, Edwin H. (1936) With Locke, H.J. *24,000 Homeless Men*, Philadelphia: J.B. Lippincott

Sutherland, Edwin H. (Ed); Conwell, Chic (pseudonym) (1937). *The Professional Thief: by a Professional Thief. Annotated and Interpreted by Edwin H. Sutherland*. Chicago: University of Chicago Press.Sutherland, Edwin H. (1942) Development of the Theory, in Karl Schuessler (ed.) *Edwin H. Sutherland on Analyzing Crime*, pp. 13-29. Chicago: University of Chicago Press.

Sutherland, Edwin H. (1949) *White Collar Crime*, New York: Holt, Rinehart & Winston.

CHAPTER 7

Johnson, Harold Whetstone; Johnston, *Mary; Names of Freedmen*; 1903, 1932; forumromanum.org

Muhammad, Elijah;_Message to the Blackman; Chapter 34; seventhfam.com

Sigmund Freud, *The Question of Lay Analysis* (Vienna 1926; English translation 1927)

Charles Rycroft, *a Critical Dictionary of Psychoanalysis* (London, 2nd Ed, 1995), p. 175

Peter Gay, *Freud: A Life for Our Time* (London 2006), p. 453

Peter Gay (ed.), *A Freud Reader* (London, 1995), p. 576

Erler, Edward J (2003), "From Subjects to citizens: The Social Origins of American Citizenship", in Pestritto, Ronald J., *the American founding and the social compact* (illustrated ed.), Lexington Books,

Erler, Edward J; Thomas G West, John A Marini (2007), *the Founders on Citizenship and Immigration: Principles and Challenges in America*, Lanham, MD: Rowman & Littlefield,

Erler, Edward J.; Thomas G. West, John A. Marini (2007),"American Citizenship and Postmodern Challenges", *the founders on citizenship and immigration: principles and challenges in America*, Rowman & Littlefield,

Mayton, William T. (2008). "Birthright Citizenship and the Civic Minimum". *Georgetown Immigration Law Journal* (Washington, D.C.: Georgetown Immigration Law Journal).

Meese, Edwin; Edwin Meese, III, David F. Forte, Matthew Spalding (2005), *the Heritage Guide to the Constitution*, Regnery Publishing,

Ridgell, Reilly (1995), *Pacific Nations and Territories: The Islands of Micronesia, Melanesia, and Polynesia*, Bess Press.

Braun, David, *Katz on Names without Bearers*, the Philosophical Review, Vol. 104, No. 4 (Oct., 1995), pp. 553–576

Coates, Richard, and "Properhood" in: Language, 82.2 (2006): 356-82

CHAPTER 8

Historian James McPherson has called it "The most eloquent expression of the new birth of freedom brought forth by reform liberalism." in McPherson, James M. *Drawn with the Sword: Reflections on the American Civil War* Oxford: Oxford University Press, 1996. p. 185. Google Book Search. Retrieved on November 27, 2007.

Wills, Garry. *Lincoln at Gettysburg.* New York: Simon & Schuster, 1992, pp. 24–25, p. 35, pp. 34–35, p. 36.

Murphy, Jim. *The Long Road to Gettysburg,* New York: Clarion Books, 1992. p. 105, "with a pronounced Kentucky accent."

"Gabor Britt, in his book *The Gettysburg Gospel,* has a thirty-page appendix that compares what Lincoln (probably) read at the memorial with what people heard and reported. Most of the differences are small, and due to understandable confusions...A few disputes seem more significant."

Greeley, Horace. *The American Conflict: A History of the Great Rebellion in the United States of America, 1860-64* Vol. I (1864)

Greeley, Horace. *Recollections of a Busy Life* (1868)

Greeley, Horace. *Essays Designed to Elucidate the Science of Political Economy, While Serving To Explain and Defend the Policy of Protection to Home Industry, As a System of National Cooperation for True Elevation of Labor,* Boston: Fields, Osgood a Co., 1870

Jonathan Elliot, Ed (1866). *The Debates in the Several State Conventions on the Adoption of the Federal Constitution, As Recommended By the General Convention at Philadelphia, In 1787.* J.B. Lippincott & Co. Washington: Taylor & Maury. pp. 237.

"A slave to the systems? Thomas Jefferson and Slavery". Hoover Institution. January 19, 2004.

Banning, Lance (August 31, 2004). "Three-Fifths Historian". The Claremont Institute.

DEDICATION

This book is dedicated to David Corona, who helped to orchestrate and bring to life the inspired words within this book. Without his foresight and his pursuit of facts, this text would not be possible.

ACKNOWLEDGMENT

This manuscript and the message that it brings would not have been possible without the help, inspiration, and dedication of many others

Special thanks to:
The founding staffers of American and Me Publishing Company and in particular Detrice Gates Howard and Yuri Rivera, for having the courage and the belief in this endeavor.

Extra special thanks to:

Armando S. Garcia, Debi Veaudry and Bill Gates, co- authors and researchers. Thanks for showing up at just the right time and knowing where to find almost anything. It was their approach in editing, which- allowed this book to reflect the majority of America's vision for a better country.